Sea Vegetable

Celebration

Shep Erhart
Leslie Cerier

Book Publishing Company
Summertown, Tennessee

© 2001 Shep Erhart, Leslie Cerier

Printed in Canada

Book Publishing Company
P.O. Box 99
Summertown, TN 38483
1-888-260-8458
www.bookpubco.com

Food styling: Barb Bloomfield, Michael Cook
Photography: Warren Jefferson
Cover design: Cynthia Holzapfel
Interior design: Gwynelle Dysmukes and Michael Cook

The following publishers have given permission for the use of these recipes: page 89, John Wiley & Sons Publishers, *Professional Vegetarian Cooking*, 1999, by Ken Bergeron; pages 84-87, 107-109, 113, and 136-137, Putnam Berkley Publishers, *Cooking the Whole Foods Way*, by Christina Pirello, 1997.

On the cover: from the bottom clockwise: Maine Spring Pasta Primavera, pages 120-121; Dulse Sushi, pages 114-115; and Dulse Chick-Pea Salad, page 88.

ISBN 1-57067-123-0

09 08 07 06 05 04 03 02 01   10 9 8 7 6 5 4 3 2 1

Library of Congress Cataloging-in-Publication Data
Erhart, Shep.
  Sea vegetable celebration / Shep Erhart, Leslie Cerier.
      p. cm.
Includes bibliographical references and index.
  ISBN 1-57067-123-0 (alk. paper)
  1. Marine algae as food. 2. Cookery (Marine algae) I.
Cerier,
Leslie. II. Title.
  TX402 .E74 2001
  641.6--dc21

2001004351

Calculations for the nutritional analyses in this book are based on the average number of servings listed with the recipes and the average amount of an ingredient if a range is called for. Calculations are rounded up to the nearest gram. If two options for an ingredient are listed, the first one is used. Not included are optional ingredients or serving suggestions.

CONTENTS

Preface

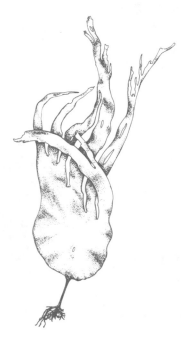

I'm glad you've followed your curiosity about sea vegetables to this book. Although it's written for someone new to the realm of edible seaweeds, those of you already familiar with these extraordinary plants undoubtedly want to know more. I believe you'll find some answers to your questions whether you're a novice, a dabbler, or a confirmed "user."

I'm hoping the information in these pages will help you accept sea vegetables as beautiful, nourishing, friendly allies in your journey to what ever makes you truly happy. I've always considered these gifts from the sea a way Mother Ocean still offers some of that "original soup" to our cells which have long memories of their birthplace. If we can receive even a fraction of the tangible and intangible nourishment in these gifts, our cells will certainly celebrate, along with our hearts and souls. And that's what I hope *Sea Vegetable Celebrations* accomplishes. This book should help you come to understand a bit more about the biology and natural intelligence of sea plants and see them as a whole food whose sum is greater than the parts, so they might contribute to your whole-health balancing act of body, mind, and spirit. We will show you how easy it is to use them in everyday cooking, how to help your family and friends enjoy them, even how to nourish your pets and plants with them.

I've been entangled in seaweed matters for over 30 years. It all started in 1971 when my wife, Linnette, leaned over a granite ledge at Schoodic Point in down East Maine and shouted, "That looks like wakame!" We found out later that it was *Alaria escalenta*, a close cousin and a fine substitute for the Japanese wakame that made up most of our miso soup each morning. We told our macrobiotic friends in Boston, and when their requests for some of the seaweed arrived, we grabbed our hip boots, baskets, and sickles and headed to the rocks at low tide. When we couldn't sun dry the seaweed, our kitchen and dining room became our wood heated "drying shed."

In 1985 Linnette, so instrumental in creating this part-time business, decided to scale back and strongly "encouraged" me to get it out of the house. For some reason I kept at it—in the barn, hiring neighbors Carl and Wendy Karush, to help with harvesting, packaging, and marketing. The business definitely became full time and took on a life of its own as well as a name—Maine Coast Sea Vegetables (MCSV). We specialize in local, indigenous plants: dulse, kelp, alaria, and laver. You'll notice a distinct bias toward these North Atlantic species in the recipe section, but we have also included information and recipes on the other varieties found in your natural food store, such as hijiki, arame, kombu, wakame, nori, agar, and sea palm.

Leslie Cerier is a very talented natural gourmet cook, author of *Quick and Easy Organic Gourmet*, and a lover of sea veggies. She has organized the wonderful recipes for this book. Leslie has a way with words, as well as with food, and lots of experience making sea veggies user friendly. She has done an excellent job of selecting and editing the best from the Maine Coast Sea Vegetables recipe files, reworking many with the help of Wendy's test kitchen.

There are also some people indirectly responsible for this book I'd like to mention here. Herman Aihara and Michio Kushi, my macrobiotic mentors, inspired me to use sea veggies daily and appreciate them as healing food. Ajaib Sing, my spiritual mentor, inspired me to make sea vegetables a livelihood and regard it as service. Key harvesters too numerous to mention from both East and West coasts have often provided the glue to allow me to stick at it, a peer support group of sorts. The core group of "old timers" at MCSV will never know how instrumental they have been in helping me keep the ship on course. And finally, none of this would have happened without communicative customers who cared enough to let me know how sea vegetables made a difference in their lives.

—Shep Erhart

MEET THE RECIPE CREATORS

Before we go any further, we would like to thank the following folks for their contributions to making sea vegetables more friendly to our American palettes and allowing us to borrow their recipes:

Linnette Erhart, who has been playing with seaweeds in the kitchen for 30 years and is the co-founder of Maine Coast Sea Vegetables.

Sharon Ann Rhodes, whose *Cooking With Sea Vegetables*, published in 1970, started many people down the seaweed path.

Eleanor Lewallen, who co-authored *The Sea Vegetable Gourmet Cookbook* with her husband John, and has been pioneering the use of seaweeds on the West Coast since the early 1970s.

Susan Asanovic, registered dietitian, gourmet cook, and teacher—a longtime Maine Coast Sea Vegetables supporter.

Christina Pirello, who authored the colorful *Cooking the Whole Foods Way*, created a natural foods cooking series for the Discovery Channel, and who knows how to make sea veggies fun and easy to use.

Ken Bergeron, an award winning vegetarian chef and author of *Professional Vegetarian Cooking* who has helped Maine Coast Sea Vegetables with professional chef recipes.

Wendy Karush, who has been teaming sea veggies with luscious land veggies from her bountiful garden for over 20 years. The best of these concoctions are in her *Good Foods* cookbook.

Peter and Montse Bradford, who produced *Cooking With Sea Vegetables*, one of the first macrobiotic cookbooks dedicated to sea veggies in England in 1985.

Sea Vegetables to Celebrate

Highlights of Your Favorite Sea Vegetables

Alaria (*Alaria esculenta* [N. Atlantic], *A. marginata* [N. Pacific])

MCSV sells this type of kelp as Alaria—Wild Atlantic Wakame. Alaria is called "edible kelp" in North America, "bladderlocks" in Scotland, and "tangle" in Ireland. It consists of beautiful, olive brown fronds (leaf-like growth that performs photosynthesis and stores nutrients) which grow from 6 to 12 feet with golden midribs. The spore-bearing leaves at the base of the plants look like wings, or "alaria" in Latin.

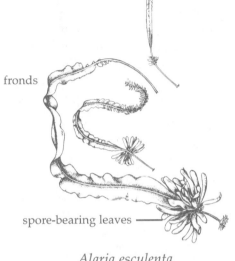

Alaria esculenta

Alaria is the perfect sea veggie for soups, particularly miso soup. (See page 75.) It's very similar to Japanese wakame but takes longer to cook (20 minutes). Alaria is great blanched, pressure cooked, soaked (24 hours), or marinated (12 hours). Nutritionally, it's comparable to whole sesame seeds as far as calcium content (1,100 mg/100 g) and has high vitamin A content (8,487 IU/100 g) similar to parsley or spinach.

Arame (*Eisenia bicyclis*, or *E. arborea* [S. Arasaki])

This is not to be confused with hiziki (*Hizikia fusiforme*). Arame looks similar but has a milder taste and texture. It has wrinkly 12-inch fronds which grow well below the low tide line in coastal Japan. Traditionally it was harvested by Japanese women divers; after harvesting it is boiled for several hours before being dried and chopped.

Arame cooks quickly and becomes very succulent. Soak it for a few minutes, and then add to any salad or dressing. You can also soak or marinate arame, and use it to spice up a stir-fry. It makes a great addition to any soup for an ocean accent. Add it while cooking grains a few minutes before the grains are finished. Arame is a great source of chelated, colloidal calcium (1,170 mg / 100 g).

Dulse (*Palmaria palmata* [formally classified as *Rhodamania palmata*])

Dulse is called "dillisk" in Ireland, "tellesk" in Brittany, and "sol" in Iceland. This should not be confused with "pepper dulse," (*Laurencia pinnatifida*, British Isles) which looks similar but has a stronger, peppery taste. Dulse thrives in cold, coastal North Atlantic and Northeast Pacific waters such as Alaska. It has reddish purple, hand-shaped fronds 6 to 12 inches long. Dulse is hand picked from the lower intertidal zone from June through September. It is then sun dried.

holdfast

Palmaria palmata

You can enjoy dulse as a nutritious chewy snack right out of the bag, or you can instantly tenderize it with a quick rinse and use it for salads and sandwiches. It cooks in 5 minutes and adds a distinct, tangy taste to soups and stir-fries. Dulse is complimentary to most potato or cheese dishes and is great with fresh fruit, salad greens, or in smoothies. You can pan-fry dulse to make tangy chips or a bacon substitute for your BLT. Kids love dulse!

Dulse's 22% protein content makes it higher in protein than chickpeas, almonds, or whole sesame seeds. It is relatively low in sodium (1,740 mg / 100 g) and high in potassium (7,820 mg / 100 g). One ounce provides 100% of the RDA for iron, fluoride, and vitamin B_6.

Hiziki (*Hizikia fusiforme*)

Hiziki is called "chin tsai" or "pigs foot vegetable" in China and "nongmichae" in Korea. These upright, many branched, blackish brown plants grow near low water in Japan and China. They are harvested when young early in the year; plants are usually par boiled before drying.

Hiziki has a unique, mild, nut-like flavor and crisp texture. To rehydrate hiziki, soak it for about 10 minutes; the plants will expand 3 to 5 times their size. Once rehydrated, they are easy to simmer, sauté, or steam with other vegetables. Hiziki turns jet black when cooked and makes an attractive garnish or side dish. After soaking, you can also marinate hiziki or serve as is or with a salad.

Hiziki has the highest calcium content of all sea veggies (1400 mg/100 g). It is high in iron (29 mg/100 g) and most B vitamins.

Kelp, *Laminaria longicruris*

MCSV sells this type of kelp as Kelp—Wild Atlantic Kombu. Kelp is also called "Atlantic kombu" or "oarweed" in America. There are many types of seaweed often called kelp. (See the endnotes for a listing of some of the most common varieties.[1])

This type of kelp loves quiet water in shallow North Atlantic bays. It grows 3- to 6-foot hollow stipes

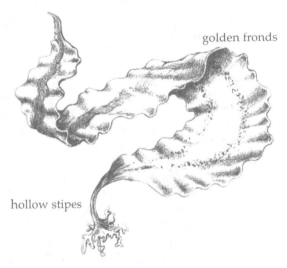

golden fronds

hollow stipes

Laminaria longicruris

(stem-like supportive tissue) and 4 to 8 foot broad, golden fronds. It is cut by hand from the subtidal zone from April through July. Kelp is hung up to dry one blade at a time!

It is the all-around sea veggie. Kelp is similar to thin Japanese kombu, but it cooks more quickly. It is great roasted, fried, pickled, boiled, sautéed, and marinated. Kelp blades are thin enough to tenderize quickly—a must for all soup stocks. Try pan frying bite-size pieces in oil for delicious "kelp chips." Never cook beans without it; kelp tenderizes, shortens cooking times, and increases digestibility.

It is exceptionally high in all major minerals, particularly calcium (942 mg/100 g), potassium (11,200 mg/100 g), magnesium (900 mg/100 g), and iron (42 mg/100 g). Kelp is also rich in important trace minerals such as manganese, copper, and zinc. One ounce provides the RDA for chromium, instrumental in blood sugar regulation. It is extremely high in iodine. (See the note on iodine intake under "Sea Vegetables and Minerals," pages 21-23.)

Kombu   (*Laminaria japonica*)

Called "kombu" in America, Europe, and Japan and "kunpu" in China, it is not to be confused with other kelp species. (See endnote 1 page 39.) It is often grown on ropes in Japan and China. Kombu is composed of ruffled fronds up to 15 feet long and 1 foot wide, growing from short solid stipes. It is usually sun dried, bundled, and pressed to flatten, then cut into 5-inch strips. Try roasting it in a 250°F oven to tenderize before crumbling it into soups, stir-fries, and salads.

Kombu is the essential sea veggie for soup stock (dashi). (See Soups page 71.) Glutamic acid, a natural MSG found in kombu, makes cooking beans quick and easy. This natural form of MSG is chemically different from manufactured MSG and is all right for people with sensitivity to manufactured MSG. Kombu's high manitol sugar content adds sweetness to its salty sea flavor. Kombu is very high in iodine.

Laver   (*Porphyra umbilicalis* or *P. leucosticta* [N. Atlantic]; *P. perforata*, or *P. nereocystis* [N. Pacific])

MCSV sells this sea vegetable as Laver— Wild Atlantic Nori. Laver is called "wild nori" in America, "purple laver" in England, "sloak" in Scotland, "karango" in New Zealand, and "chichoy" in China. It should not be confused with the plant commonly known

Porphyra umbilicalis

as "nori" (*P. yezoeonsis, P. tenera*) which is grown on floating nets and processed into sheets.

Laver is found in the upper to mid-intertidal zone in colder Northern and Southern Hemisphere waters. It looks like grayish black popped balloons hanging off of rocks or rockweed. The small, stipeless circular fronds are easy to dry in the sun from May through September.

Lightly roasting laver enhances its flavor and tenderizes it. Laver has a nutty, almost sweet taste due to the amino acids or protein it contains. Roasted laver is great crumbled into soups, grains, salads, and popcorn. Once it is boiled down to a purée, it is called "laver bread" in Scotland and Wales. It was eaten by 18th century whalers to prevent scurvy.

Laver is a good source of protein (28 to 30%), chelated manganese (3.4 mg / 100 g), zinc (4.1 mg / 100 g), copper (.612 mg / 100 g), and fluoride (5.8 mg / 100 g). It is also high in most B vitamins, vitamin C (12 mg / 100 g), and vitamin E.

Nori   (*Porphya yezonesis, Porphya tenera* [N. Pacific])

Nori should not be confused with "wild nori" or "laver" (see laver page 10) or "aonori" (*Monostroma latissiima*), a green flaked sea veggie from Japan.

Hybridized nori plants spore in tanks. The plants mature on suspended nets. Once harvested, they are chopped into a slurry and processed into a paper-like consistency for making into sheets. Japan, China, and Korea produce billions of sheets during the October to April season.

Nori was traditionally used only for sushi; it is now used to wrap anything for finger food. It has a mild, nutty, sweet taste, which is easy for anyone new to sea vegetables (even kids) to like. Nori must be toasted to bring out its flavor. Most of the nori now sold in stores is pretoasted. It is great slivered or crumbled over grains, stir-fries, soups, pasta, or salads. Nori makes a tasty, nutritious snack as is, right out of the bag.

Nori has the highest protein content of any sea veggie—up to 35%. It is the highest of all sea veggies in vitamin A and vitamin C and the lowest in iodine content. It has a good supply of all the B vitamins.

Sea Palm   (*Postelsia palmaeformis*)

Sea palm has 2-foot, upright rigid stipes topped with hanging corrugated fronds—like little palm trees. Its long, thin, grooved blades look very much like a pasta. It thrives in the most turbulent surf of intertidal Northeast Pacific waters. It is harvested by hand in small quantities from April through June. Only part of the hanging fronds are cut to insure regrowth and sustainability.

Sea palm has a very mild taste for a sea vegetable, with a texture that is soft and crunchy.

Presoaking reduces the cooking time considerably. Roasting in a low oven tenderizes and enhances the flavor. You can mix roasted fronds with almonds and walnuts for a great snack. You can also marinate sea palm overnight and add it to a salad or try as is.

There is no nutritional information available for sea palm.

Wakame   (*Undaria pinnatifida*)

Wakame has dark brown fronds 12 to 16 inches wide and 2 to 4 feet long. It is often blanched or par boiled to tenderize it before drying.

It should not be confused with alaria (*Alaria esculenta* [N. Atlantic] or *A. marginata* [N. Pacific])—wild plants resembling wakame with narrower fronds and tougher midribs. Wakame is now mostly cultivated off the northern coasts of Japan, particularly Hokaido.

It has a very mild taste and soft texture with a slightly crisp midrib. Wakame cooks more quickly than alaria, including the midrib. It is the traditional sea veggie for miso soup, but is also great in any long-cooking soup. You can marinate it for salads or add it to a sandwich.

Wakame is second only to hiziki in calcium (1,300 mg/100 g). If you are iodine sensitive, wakame is relatively low in iodine (3 mg/100 g).

What are Sea Vegetables and Where do They Come From?

Out of the sea "soup" of our Earth's early oceans arose single-celled organisms that changed everything—algae (probably blue-green algae). Their ability to transform the sun's energy, the sea's water, and the Earth's minerals into organic carbohydrates, fats, and proteins provided the basic "meal" for all higher life forms. The addition of oxygen from their photosynthesis into the earth's atmosphere eventually supported complex animals like us. Fossil records show that vast quantities of these early algae thrived three billion years ago.

Today there are about 65,000 species of algae still with us; 20,000 of those species still live in the ocean. Only a hundred or so species are consumed by humans. In this book you will get to know a dozen or so of the macroalgae, the big brown, green, and red ones you find dried in your natural food store or that you might see on the seashore.

Sea vegetables grow in the highly energized zone where liquid meets solid, deep and dark meets light and air, and where rollers generated in storms off Cape Cod thunder onto Maine granite. What kind of energy imprint would this leave on a plant that is anchored on the bedrock yet is exposed to each breaking wave? If you could see these graceful plants breaking with the waves, words might come to mind such as resilient, tenacious, supple, flexible, and above all, beautiful. In my opinion, these energetic and aesthetic qualities are part of the intangible benefits your cells receive when you chose to eat sea vegetables.

A Quick Trip Down to the Ocean's Edge

The intertidal zone is an immensely fertile arena where the land's organic and mineral matter meets the ocean's mighty mixing of water and sunlight. This is where most seaweed flourishes. Let's say you're in Maine. It's June and low tide. Leaving the safe footing of granite rocks, you step onto a slippery, thick carpet of olive brown rockweed made up of two typical macroalgae from the brown algae family (*Fucus vasiculosis* and *Ascophyllum nodosum*). They cling to the

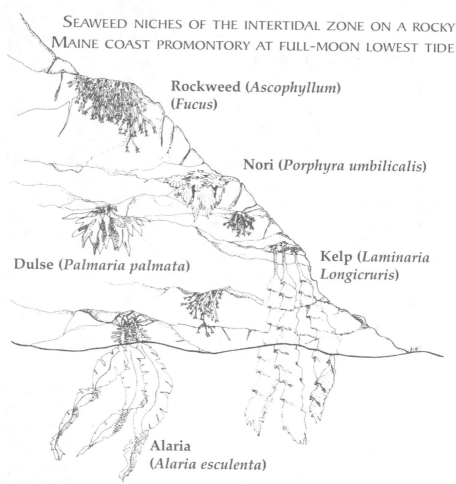

Rockweed (*Ascophyllum*)
(*Fucus*)

Nori (*Porphyra umbilicalis*)

Dulse (*Palmaria palmata*)

Kelp (*Laminaria Longicruris*)

Alaria
(*Alaria esculenta*)

granite with "holdfasts," root-like anchoring devices. From these grow short round "stipes," stem-like supportive tissue. These stipes lead to "fronds," leaf-like growth that performs photosynthesis and stores nutrients. As you might have guessed by now, internal nutrient transport is not necessary for these plants because they are bathed in nutrients as soon as the tide comes in.

Keeping themselves bathed in light for photosynthesis, however, is their challenge. This rockweed has met it in at least two ways. First, its brown pigmentation allows absorption of the shorter blue and green wavelengths of light that can penetrate the fifteen feet of water at high tide. It has also grown various small bladders on the fronds to keep it floating off the bottom, facilitating both light and nutrient gathering. The rockweed is made up of *Fucus* and *Ascophyllum*, not plants you'll be cooking with, but which are commonly found in both nutritional supplements, such as "kelp" or "bladderwrack," and also in plant and animal foods labeled "rockweed," "kelp," or "seaweed meal."

At the upper edge of this rockweed carpet you might also notice a 3- to 5-inch, leaf-like green algae called *Ulva letuca*. This plant is almost all frond, with no stipe and a tiny holdfast. It looks like lettuce and is commonly called "sea lettuce." It doesn't taste like lettuce at all, being much tougher and a lot saltier. It's commonly eaten in Asia as aonori and is available from some West Coast suppliers (see Resources, page 156). Or you could easily spread some on a rock in the sun to dry.

Laver (*Porphyra*) is another macroalgae you might notice in this upper zone. It looks very much like a popped balloon. You'll find it at your feet amongst the rockweed or on a protruding rock face. The color of this hand-sized seaweed ranges from light gray to very dark purple or black, depending on the species and the season. This is the plant that Maine Coast Sea Vegetables sells as laver (its common name in the British Isles), or wild Atlantic nori. From these wild *Porphyra* species the Japanese selectively bred the cultivated plants they process into nori sheets, the black wrappers for sushi.[2]

These ingenious *Porphyra* plants are part of the red algae family that masks their green chlorophyll with red pigments, so they can live deeper where only blue-green light waves penetrate. When the tides roll in, you will see these popped balloons spring to life in the currents and fluoresce deep purples and reds.

The tide is more than halfway out now, so let's carefully meander a bit further down this intertidal zone and meet another well-known "red." This one, dulse (*Palmaria palmata*), definitely looks the part, with a deep, dark red hue when exposed and a gorgeous fluorescing red sparkle when covered. You'll notice some dulse tucked in the rockweed but you'll also see lots of this hand-sized plant covering boulders, crammed into granite cracks, or hanging from sheer rock faces. It loves good wave action and has larger, stronger holdfasts than laver. If you pick some to taste, the holdfast will probably stay behind, and you'll experience a very chewy, very exciting explosion of briny tastes in your mouth.[3] It becomes more tender after drying and aging awhile.

It's now absolute low tide, lower than normal actually, because it happens to be the full moon in June. Right at the water's edge lies several of the big "browns," or *Laminaria*, as they're often referred to.[4] Nowadays, "kelp" usually refers to specific brown macroalgae— all large, land-plant-like algae, with pronounced stipes and fronds, and brown pigment which allows them to perform photosynthesis in deep water. On the U.S. Atlantic coast *Laminaria longicruris*, *Laminaria sacharina*, and *Laminaria digitata* are all sold as kelp. *Alaria esculenta*, although sometimes called "edible kelp," is actually quite distinct from these other species, having a milder taste, a mid-rib down the frond, and spore-bearing leaves (sporaphylls) at the base of the main frond. On the U.S. Pacific coast there are also sea vegetables which are sold as kelp, bull kelp, or giant kelp (*L. digitata*, *Nereocystis*, and *Macrocystis*res, respectively). In Japan different varieties of kelp are sold as kombu (their generic word for kelp). These include *Laminaria japonica* as well as four or five other *Laminaria* species.

Pick up a piece of kelp, let's say *Laminaria longicruris*, scrape off some of its slippery skin, and put it under your hand lens. You'll see tiny brown spores ready to ride the currents as they develop into male and female microorganisms that eventually "marry," settle down (to the bottom), and produce offspring during the winter to grow into next summer's kelp. By the way, these spores are rich in proteins and essential fatty acids. You may notice them when you soak your dried kelp from MCSV as a thick, dark part of the kelp frond. They are great for soup stock.

Before leaving this low tide zone, look closely at your feet to spot some Irish moss (*Chondrus crispus*). It's only 2 to 3 inches tall, very bushy, and dark black with flashes of iridescent purple, telling us it belongs to the "red" family. Boiling these beauties yields carrageenan, a gelatinous polysaccharide, valued worldwide as an emulsifier and stabilizer. You can use it to make pudding.

Now let's briefly follow the tide out on a northern California shore in June. After we climb down those Pacific palisades, some rockweed (*Fucus*) might still be under our feet, but the Pacific surge is too strong for tender *Ascophyllum* to survive here. We might also find some green sea lettuce (*Ulva*) and then some reddish wild nori

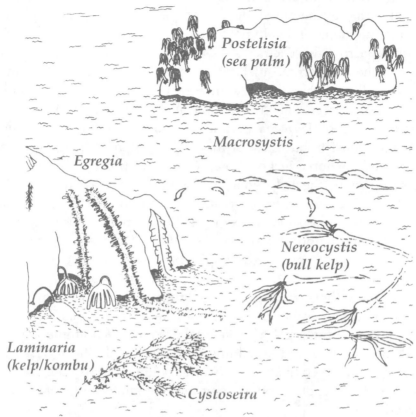

(*Porphyra*) but very little, if any, dulse. There is a look-a-like called *Iridea*, but it does not taste the same.

As the tide drops, a remarkable plant appears on rocky outcrops looking like tiny, droopy, brown palm trees. This is sea palm (*Postelsia palmaeformis*). On first seeing these beautifully, curious plants with Kate and Larry of Rising Tide Sea Vegetables in Mendocino, California, I was struck by their stoic, upright stance in small clusters on headlands that took the full brunt of the Pacific rollers—great food for perseverance and patience.

When the tide is completely out, huge beds of "kelps" undulate on the surface or just below. *Alaria* and *L. digitata* look familiar, but unique is bull kelp (*Neurosystis*), with its huge single bladder bearing dreadlock fronds. Close by is another kelp *Macrosystis* with its numerous bladders and wide blades branching off of very long stipes, allowing it to grow in water over 100 feet deep. These are plants that can regenerate a foot of frond per day and are mostly harvested for alginates and kelp powders.

Leaping across the Pacific to the outgoing tide on the shores of Hokaido, the northernmost island of Japan, we might also find the rockweed (*Fucus*) carpet with some sea lettuce (*Ulva*), along with another leafy green called *Monostromata* or aonori in Japanese. Several species of *Porphyra* or nori would be abundant, as wild plants still flourish, but most of the *Porphyra* here is hanging from floating nets anchored just offshore, waiting for processing into nori sheets. Down in the kelp zone, we would not find the familiar *Laminaria digitata* or *Laminaria sacharina*, but a new species, *Laminaria japonica*, whose long single blade we eat as kombu. And instead of *Alaria* we might find some wakame (*Undaria pinnatifida*), a long brown frond with a mid-rib and sporaphylls, somewhat similar to *Alaria*.

Deep below the surface grow two other important brown algae species that seem to be unique to the Western Pacific. There are *Eisenia arborea*, growing 2 to 10 feet tall, from which arame is produced after boiling and shredding, and the much shorter *Hizikia fusiforme*, from which hijiki is made after boiling and drying.

So there's a taste of the physiology, biology, and ecology of certain seaweeds.

A Brief History of the Use of Seaweed or Who's Been Eating Seaweed Over the Years

Let's start relatively close to home with a great story from John Lewallen of Mendocino Sea Vegetable Company in northern California. In the early 1970s, he met and got to know Laura Somersol, an elder of the northwest Indian Kashaya tribe. She told him her people had been harvesting wild nori, ("mei bil" or "sea leaf") for centuries along the Pacific coast. The whole tribe would camp near the sea leaf-covered rocks in early spring and gather and dry a year's supply of the young sea leaf that would later be deep-fried into nutritious, crispy meals.[5] There is also evidence that Native peoples on the Atlantic coast harvested and dried certain seaweeds, particularly kelp stipes.

B. J. Chapman in his great book, *Seaweeds and Their Uses*, places the earliest mentioned use of seaweed as a human food in a Chinese book of poetry from 600 B.C. A few hundred years later, several species were specifically referred to as medicinal in an ancient Chinese medical text.

The Vikings were known to carry some form of dried seaweed on long voyages for sustenance. And early New England whalers chewed on seaweed for its vitamin C to keep away scurvy. In Iceland, dulse or "sol" was prescribed as part of a school menu in the early 1700s.[6]

The Hawaiians traditionally consumed many species of *limu* (or sea vegetables) according to Magruder and Hunt in *Seaweeds of Hawaii*. These valued marine algae were even used in certain cere-monies, and sea vegetable "gardens" were maintained for royalty. Nowadays 20 species are still used, but the tradition and cultural knowledge are fading.[7]

To a lesser degree this traditional use of seaweeds in daily diet is also waning in urban Japan. More than any other culture, the Japanese have embraced and developed the role of sea vegetables as a staple food. Seiban Arasaki, in *Vegetables From the Sea*, gives a wonderfully detailed evolution of the Japanese romance with these plants. Ten thousand-year-old evidence of its use has been found in burial mounds and peat bogs from prehistoric Japan. In the 6th century kombu was part of a tribute offered by Japanese envoys visiting a Chinese court. In 8th century religious rituals, seaweed figured prominently at various shrines. Even today Arasaki lists a number of shrines where seaweed is incorporated into ceremonies. Early Chinese poetry tells us that even courtiers gathered seaweed "just as all people living by the sea considered this one of their everyday chores."[8]

This gathering of wild plants is not happening much in Japan today. But they have perfected cultivation techniques for wakame, kombu, and nori which have actually increased their overall production, much of it for export. They have also exported these cultivation techniques to China, Korea, and other Asian countries that consume sea vegetables in large quantities. The cultivation of Asian edible seaweed is a growing, multibillion-dollar industry.

Several hundred years ago, a new wave of sea veggie lovers arrived in North America from Ireland, Scotland, and Wales. They brought with them their Old World taste for oarweeds (kelp), bladderlochs (*Alaria*), dillisk (dulse), and sloak (*Porphyra*, nori, or laver).

Every time we choose to include sea vegetables in our meal, we are joining a long tradition and helping to write a new chapter in this ancient history.

What's So Healthy About Sea Vegetables?

This family of plants that has been beneficial to many cultures for centuries possesses some extraordinary healing elements and offers substantial nutritional value. In the next few pages, we'll explore the unique qualities of seaweed vitamins, minerals, protein, fiber, and fats.

There is still a lot we do not know about sea vegetables. Unfortunately, not much rigorous scientific research or clinical studies have been done so far. But fortunately, there are centuries of empirical and anecdotal evidence of seaweeds' effectiveness. Here are a couple of examples.

West Coast seaweed pioneer Evelyn McConnaughey, in her book *Sea Vegetables* (Naturegraph, 1985), has thoughtfully organized some of the evidence in "Marine Algae in Modern and Folk Medicine." She has gathered worldwide references to seaweed being used successfully in the treatment of goiter, kidney disease, ulcers, nausea, obesity, high blood pressure, constipation, menstrual disorders, cancer, hypertension, worms, high cholesterol, arteriolosclerosis, hypoglycemia, and more.

In a book called *Kelp, The Health Giver*, Dr. Eric Powell, Ph.D., N.D., documents case histories from his practice in England in the 1960s and '70s, giving detailed descriptions of using a type of kelp (*Fucus*) to treat headaches, high blood pressure, indigestion, obesity, rheumatism, bronchitis, and other types of glandular disorders.[9]

If you're looking for more scientific evidence, some interesting reports of research being done worldwide are found in the following section. And more scientific literature on completed research is turning up every day on the internet, particularly from Asia where seaweed is more important as a food source. Even in this country, researchers like Jane Teas have found funding for clinical studies using *Alaria* (see Cancer, pages 29-30). Just recently I was contacted by a researcher from Ryerson University in Toronto for a supply of dulse to continue her preliminary, promising investigations into its antioxidant properties.

Sea Vegetables and Minerals

Every second of every day your body depends on minerals to generate billions of tiny electric impulses throughout your nervous system. Your heart would stop, your muscles would freeze, and your brain would black out if these minerals were not available in just the right amounts and the right form. The minerals in seaweeds are in colloidal form, meaning they retain their molecular identity while remaining in liquid suspension. Colloids are very small in size and are easily absorbed by the body's cells. Plants convert metallic minerals, which can be toxic, into colloids with a natural, negative electric charge. Negatively charged minerals have been shown to increase the transport and bioavailability of other foods and supplements.[10]

Minerals that are attached to other substances such as amino acids are also more bioavailable. These are called chelated (key-lated) minerals, from the Greek word for claw. Seaweeds provide all of the 56 minerals and trace minerals required for your body's physiological functions in chelated, colloidal forms. Most enzymatic functions depend on minute amounts of bioavailable trace minerals. The major minerals are instrumental in all kinds of life-sustaining activities in your body: magnesium is crucial in calcium absorption, iodine in thyroid function, iron in blood oxygen exchange, and chromium in blood sugar regulation. All of these functions are facilitated by the presence of chelated, colloidal minerals.

Alex Jack, in *Let Food Be Thy Medicine*, has noticed in the latest (1997) USDA "Food Composition Handbook," a decline in vitamin and mineral content between 25 and 50% since the last survey done in 1975. For example, random sampling of 12 garden vegetables showed an average decline of 26.5% in calcium. The handbook concludes, "This (decline) suggests a steady deterioration in soil, air, and water quality as well as reduced seed vitality that is depleting minerals and other inorganic compounds from our food."

And where does all this mineral-depleted soil end up—the ocean, where seaweeds incorporate them into chelated, colloidal compounds ready for our mineral-deprived bodies. Population studies show that people with diets high in sea vegetables have few symptoms of mineral depletion and their life spans are longer. [11] Take a look at the nutrition chart in on pages 154-155 and you can see why.

Finally a cautionary note about getting too much of a good mineral, namely iodine. We all need between 150 and 1,100 micrograms in our daily diets to keep our thyroids functioning properly.[12] But some people with sensitive thyroids, particularly nursing mothers or postmenopausal women, may have adverse reactions to excess iodine. Some seaweeds, particularly kelp, provide extraordinary amounts of iodine. Healthy thyroids will "spill" excess iodine, but only you or your health practitioner can be the judge. So far at MCSV we have never had a complaint, but it's important to note one of the few possible downsides of eating too much of these great plants.

Sea Vegetables and Protein

The protein content of most edible sea vegetables ranges from 10 to 48%. Arasaki says in his book *Vegetables From the Sea* that "amino acids in these (seaweed) proteins are about the same as those in ordinary proteins, and the amino acid composition is actually better than that of land plants. Interestingly, this amino acid composition closely resembles egg white protein."[13] (Egg protein is considered the most utilizable by the human body.)

Unlike certain grains and beans that are lacking one or two of the essential amino acids, most sea vegetables contain all of the essential amino acids and may be a good complement to grains and beans for making complete-protein meals. For example, the yellow corn in MCSV Sea Chips is low in tryptophan and threonine, but the kelp and dulse seasonings on the chips provide both of them, allowing your body to form a complete protein from the combination.

There's also nonprotein nitrogen available in seaweeds from free amino acids, peptides, amines, and nucleotides. One of the more important aminos in the big brown seaweeds is glutamic acid, the basis for synthetic MSG. This is why kelps naturally enhance flavors and tenderize high-protein foods like beans while also aiding in their digestion.

Sea Vegetables and Fats

Sea veggies are good food for people on diets. Different types of kelp are often found in weight loss formulas. They add little fat or calories, and the extra iodine stimulates the thyroid to burn more fat. The extra fiber aids digestion. Sea vegetables contain only 1 to 2% fat. This fat is mostly unsaturated.

Several years ago I had three of our big brown seaweeds tested for their concentrations of omega-6 and omega-3 essential fatty acids at the University of Maine. The ratio of the omega-6 to omega-3 was a favorable 2 to 1 and 3 to 2. The NIH (based on their "Acceptable Intakes") suggests a ratio of omega-6 to omega-3 between 2 to 1 and 3 to 1. As a vegetable source of essential fatty acids, microalgae (spirulina, chlorella, etc.) are richer, but the brown macroalgae might be at least making a contribution to your body's need for these essential fats. They will certainly contribute magnesium, selenium, zinc, and vitamins A, carotene, B_3, B_6, C, and E—the required nutrients for optimum utilization of omega-3 and omega-6 fatty acids.[4]

Sea Vegetables and Vitamins

Many edible sea vegetables contain significant amounts of vitamin A in the form of beta-carotene. Nori (*Porphyra*), for example, tests in a range from 20,400 to 44,500 International Units, depending on the species and processing.[15] Other sea veggies, such as alaria and kelp, yield considerable amounts of B_1, B_2, B_3, and B_6. Some freshly harvested or carefully dried seaweed, such as laver, show high amounts of vitamin C or vitamin E. Please refer to the nutrition chart on pages 154-155. Remember these numbers are relative to many factors such as harvest season, drying procedures, storage/packaging, and your preparation.

The Controversy Over Vitamin B_{12}

Then there is the ongoing debate over vitamin B_{12}, which shows up in small quantities in many seaweeds, using several different types of analyses.[16] But is it really vitamin B_{12} or an analogue (something which appears to be B_{12} but is not able to be used by the body)? Is it really available to the body at all when eaten as seaweed? These are questions that have no definitive answer because a controlled clinical study has yet to be done using seaweed as the sole source of vitamin B_{12}.

B_{12} is produced by bacteria and is usually found only in animals. So where could this supposed B_{12} come from? Two researchers in Great Britain published a study on dulse in 1954 to confirm the concentration of cobalt from seawater as vitamin B_{12} or cyanocobalamin in the seaweed. They were unsuccessful in establishing exactly how dulse produced the B_{12}, but confirmed it was there and speculated it was made, "perhaps by bacteria living in the surrounding seawater or on the surface of the plant."

There is even controversy over the most accurate testing procedure for B_{12} in plant material. Maine Coast Sea Vegetables started testing for B_{12} back in the mid-1970s and found some in all of its sea vegetables. Because of the controversy over testing, MCSV retested all of its sea vegetables for B_{12} using a new method in 1991.[17] In most cases, the total B_{12} reported was even greater than that reported with the original method. See nutrition chart, pages 154-155.

If the metabolically active B_{12} is available, how well can the human body use it? This is still a hot topic.[18] What is missing in all these discussions is an extensive (and costly) clinical trial; something we have tried to organize through MCSV but have never found the funding to pull off.

Meanwhile, I look to more empirical evidence of B_{12} activity in my own body, having eaten no meat or fish or even much cheese in the last 30 years, but lots of seaweed. I've never shown symptoms of B_{12} deficiency, nor has my wife or daughter who was born and raised, and still is, a conscientious vegetarian. There is also Dr. Sherry Rogers' experience with her vegan patients who only showed low B_{12} levels in blood tests when they hadn't been eating the sea vegetables she had prescribed.[19] What can I say? You obviously have to decide for yourself.

Sea Vegetables and Fiber

According to The Nutrition Desk Reference (New Canaan: Keats Publishing, 1995), dietary fiber is any substance that remains essentially undigested by the time it reaches the large intestine. By this definition, many seaweeds are a great source of dietary fiber as they contain unique colloidal carbohydrates that are not broken down with stomach acids or enzymes and are not absorbed in the small intestines. Fibrous materials in seaweeds are like pectin, gums, or hemicelluloses in land plants, in that they have the ability to absorb water.

Maine Coast Sea Vegetables tested four of its primary North Atlantic seaweeds for both soluble and insoluble dietary fibers in 1989 and found they were all considered high-fiber sources. Most of them were above 30% total dietary fiber. (Oat bran is about 30%; dulse is about 33% dietary fiber.) Does this mean that all the claims made for high-fiber foods can be made for seaweeds? Unfortunately the research and clinical studies are yet to be done, but there is some interesting information available on some of this fibrous material.

For example, alginates, typical in the big brown kelps (*Laminaria*), are extracted world wide for use in many industrial, medical, and food technology applications. They are discussed as important detoxifiers in the section "Sea Vegetables and Radiation," pages 30-31. Fucoidan, a polysaccharide, is proven to have the same anticoagulant action as heparin (another polysaccharide with anticoagulant action found in the tissues of animals).[20] Russian researchers extracted a similar polysaccharide, U-Fucoidan, that proved to be an excellent absorber of heavy metals and radioactive elements.[21] A news release from Japan states that, "Takara (laboratory) has discovered that the polysaccharide known as F-Fucoidan, contained in kombu and other brown seaweeds, can significantly enhance production of Hepatocyte Growth Factor (HGF) in a laboratory setting. HGF has been shown to enhance the growth and regeneration not only of liver cells but also of vascular cells, heart cells, and cartilage."[22]

Perhaps the best known of all the functional dietary fibers in seaweed is carrageenan, extracted mostly from Irish moss (*Chondrus crispus*) but also from several other large, red sea vegetables. It is widely used in the food processing industry as a stabilizer, emulsifier, filler, etc. You've eaten it often in ice cream and chocolate pudding; even the head on your beer might be augmented with a little carrageenan. But it also has a wide use in traditional medicine for any ailment of the intestines and for respiratory problems.

And finally, one of the dietary fibers you might have already tried, or may wish to try using one of the recipes in this book, is agar or kantan, as it is called in Japan. This complex carbohydrate is extracted from the cell walls of a number of red seaweeds. The agar you buy in the store dissolves in hot water and congeals slowly as it cools. It is a nutritious alternative to gelatin which is made from animal hooves. It's used as a medium for growing bacterial cultures, as few bacteria can decompose it. It is also used widely in cosmetics.

Using Sea Vegetables as a Medicinal Botanical

Sea Vegetables and Heart Disease

Traditional Oriental medicine has long held that the use of seaweeds lowers the risk of heart disease. It should be no surprise that recent research on some kelps (*Ascophyllum* and *Fucus*) have shown their ability to lower plasma cholesterol levels.[23]

In his book, *Vegetables From the Sea*, Dr. Seiban Arasaki identifies five different studies of how seaweed or seaweed extracts have been found to lower blood plasma cholesterol in animals and/or humans. Kombu (*Laminaria*), nori (*Porphyra*), Irish moss (*Chondrus*), and bladderwrack (*Fucus*) are among the species mentioned in these studies. He also mentions a study by Professor S. Kado of Tohoku University who found that people living in areas of Japan that ate the most seaweed had the greatest life spans and lowest heart failures often associated with high plasma cholesterol levels.[24]

Doctor Zakir Ramazanov, writing in *Nutraceuticals World*, states, "Sea vegetables have been shown to lower significantly plasma cholesterol levels and the active compounds have been identified: Fucosterol, and the unsaturated fatty acids show hypocholesterolemic activity. This ability to reduce plasma cholesterol levels and to increase serum lipolytic activity may explain their use in the prevention of arteriolosclerosis."[25]

And there's another good reason to eat your sea veggies—potassium. The FDA has just authorized this health claim, "Diets containing foods that are a good source of potassium and low in sodium may reduce the risk of high blood pressure and stroke." Check out the potassium levels on page 154. Do yourself and your heart a favor, and find more ways to include these remarkable plants in your daily diet.

Sea Vegetables and Hypertension

There are several possible explanations why seaweed has been successfully used to treat hypertension. Dr. Seiban Arasaki states that an extract of kombu made by immersing the seaweed in water at 140°F and steeping it for 5 to 24 hours at room temperature, "provides a parallel reduction of both maximum and minimum blood pressures. In 1964 Dr. Takamoto identified the amino acid Laminine as the effective hypertensive element in *Laminaria japonica* (kombu)."[26]

Back in the late 60s in England, Dr. Eric Powell, Ph.D., N.D., successfully treated patients suffering from hypertension with *Fucus*, which he called kelp. In his theory he stated, "Kelp has a normalizing action upon the thyroid and parathyroid . . . Better function of the parathyroid glands means that the system can take up and utilize mineral matter to the best advantage: in particular calcium, iodine, and sodium which all play a part in maintaining the health and elasticity of the arterial walls."[27]

Debra Ahern, Ph.D., R.D., reporting her findings in the *Journal of the American Dietetic Association*, sees it a little differently. It is well known to dieticians that people with low blood potassium levels are more prone to hypertension. Dr. Ahern maintained that seaweed-based seasonings provide not only high concentrations of potassium but also chloride, a means of retaining this potassium. In her study she says, "Chloride may play an indirect positive role in hypertension by allowing renal retention of potassium. If this is the case, potassium sources that provide chloride may be more effective in raising blood plasma levels than fruits and vegetables. The high chloride content of those seasonings with seaweed may make them good sources of potassium for clients at risk of hypokalemia (too little potassium)."[28]

And finally, an article, "Blood Pressure and Nutrient Intake," from *U.S. Science* magazine states that higher intakes of calcium, potassium, and sodium are associated with lower mean systolic pressure and lower absolute risk of hypertension.[29] Sea vegetables supply extraordinary amounts of sodium, potassium, and calcium in easy-to-assimilate, organic molecular compounds. Check the nutritional analysis chart on pages 154-155, and you will have to agree that seaweeds' greatest strength is as a premium source of minerals.

Sea Vegetables and Cancer

Sea vegetables have been used for centuries in Japanese and Chinese medicine for treatment of cancer. Some recent scientific research has started to verify this traditional usage. For example, a study in 1995 demonstrated antitumor activity in kelp (*Ascophyllum* and *Fucus*) against leukemia P-388. Certain compounds in kombu (*Laminaria japonica*) and wakame (*Andaria pinnatifida*) have been shown to have antimutagenic activity. Fucons (sulfated polysaccharides) extracted from brown seaweeds or kelps have been shown to inhibit cell growth, which means they may be able to inhibit the growth of cancer cells.[30]

But perhaps the most exciting work with cancer and seaweeds has been done by Jane Teas who is affiliated with Interdisciplinary Programs and Health at the Harvard School of Public Health. In 1981 she published a paper on a number of well-documented reasons why the consumption of seaweed, particularly the kelps, was a factor in the lower rate of breast cancer found in postmenopausal women in Japan. The paper is technical but the abstract is easy to follow and may entice you to read the original, so I quote it in full:

"Based on epidemiological (study of populations) and biological data, *Laminaria*, a brown kelp seaweed, is proposed as an important factor contributing to the relatively low breast cancer rates reported in Japan. Several possible mechanisms for the influence of *Laminaria* on breast cancer are proposed: *Laminaria* is a source of nondigestible fiber, thereby increasing fecal bulk and decreasing bowel transit time; it changes the post hepatic metabolism of sterols; it contains an antibiotic substance that may influence fecal ecology; it contains 1-3 beta glucan, which alters enzymatic activity of fecal flora, and it stimulates the host mediated immune response. It is suggested that *Laminaria* may play a role in preventing either the initiation of breast cancer or its promotion by endogenous physiological factors."[31]

After gathering so much evidence of seaweeds' multifaceted anti-carcinogenic properties, Jane decided to conduct a clinical trial of 25 postmenopausal women from the Boston-Amherst area which is continuing today. The seaweed she is using is *Alaria* harvested from the Maine coast by Larch Hanson of Maine Seaweed Company. She is hoping to prove that *Alaria* (and other brown macroalgae) provide enough phytoestrogen material to have the effect of estrogen replacement therapy. The early test results look promising, but the research has not yet been published or offered for peer review.

Finally, Dr. Andrew Weil in his newsletter recently stated, "Scientists at the National Cancer Institute are now investigating the anticancer properties of seaweeds, including one found off the coast of Curaçao that appears to be more potent than Taxol."[32] I'm not sure what seaweeds are under study, but it's safe to say that the National Cancer Institute would not be evaluating them if they had not already demonstrated some anticarcinogenic properties.

Sea Vegetables and Radiation

The first studies on fighting radiation poisoning with seaweed were started 30 years ago at McGill University in Montreal, Canada. Researchers found that alginic acid, one of the important intercellular polysaccharides found in big brown algae like kelp and alaria, could reduce the amount of strontium 90 absorbed through the intestinal wall.[33] Later research established that this alginate formed strong bonds with both free and embedded radioactive nuclides and heavy metals in the human gastrointestinal tract. No enzymatic or intestinal bacterial action could break these bonds so that the toxic material was passed safely out of the body.[34]

J.F. Stera of the EPA reported similar results from the EPA's Environmental Toxicology Laboratory. "Our investigation has shown that alginate (from kelp) can bind radioactive strontium 90, one of the most hazardous pollutants, effectively in the gastrointestinal tract, thus preventing its absorption into the body. And it now shows that alginate bonds with other metal pollutants such as excess bromium, cadmium, and zinc." Stera also observed how strontium, already stored in the bones, was resecreted and bound by the alginic acid forming strontium alginate which was safely excreted in the stool.[35]

Another prevalent and toxic element, radioactive Iodine 131, accumulates in the thyroid gland. Steven Schechter, in *Fighting Radiation with Seaweed*, observes, "If sufficient amounts of natural iodine are available, radioactive iodine will not be absorbed." He recommends seaweed as the source for that natural iodine.[36] Kelp has the highest amount of iodine of any seaweed.

Ara Der Marderosian writes in the *Journal of Pharmaceutical Sciences* that sodium alginate from kelp reduces the uptake of strontium 90 from the gastrointestinal tract by a factor of nine. And, "The use of sodium alginate appears to be able to remove this contaminant (SR 90) without seriously affecting the availability of calcium, sodium, or potassium to the body."[37]

After the Chernobyl nuclear meltdown in Russia, we noticed a rise in kelp sales at Maine Coast Sea Vegetables. We joined with other small producers from both coasts to send a CARE package of brown algae to the survivors of the region. I have also learned that the Russians used this nuclear accident as the impetus to start serious research into the use of their kelps from Vladivlostok, from which they isolated the polysaccharide U-Fucoidan, an excellent absorber of radioactive elements. Seaweeds' effectiveness in treating radiation and heavy metal poisoning is well documented and well known worldwide.

Sea Vegetables as Whole Food

Let's consider the merits of these marine plants as more than their parts, as a whole, living food. This perspective is more soulful than scientific, more intuitive than analytical. Our cells and those of seaweed are both bathed in a similar ocean of dissolved mineral matter. The ratio of sodium to potassium is nearly the same in blood and seawater. Our cells and the cells of seaweed both contain similar complex metabolic mechanisms and use similar building blocks of amino acids, polysaccharides, fats, enzymes, etc. So when we eat a whole plant, we automatically get the broad assortment of nutrients and phytochemicals that our cells require. As Dr. Donald Davis puts it in his newsletter "Health Hunter": "The biochemical unity of all nature serves as the nutritional foundation of all creation."[38]

In other words, perhaps it's not necessary to worry about what's in seaweed, or what it's good for. You can eat a particular sea veggie because of a particular nutrient or health benefit it provides, or you can eat it because it looks beautiful, smells good, feels right, and tastes great. Either way you can't go wrong!

Nourishing Animals with Sea Vegetables

Over the years at Maine Coast Sea Vegetables, I have received interesting anecdotes from customers who have fed seaweed to their house pets. For example Cynthia Olsen writes, "I was munching on some of your wonderful dulse the other day, when my dog begged for some too. I didn't think she would eat it. Imagine my surprise when she chomped it down and asked for more." From Mary we have this story, "Just wanted you to know that we love your products and we use the sea veggies to feed our tropical marine fish. They love the dulse and inhale the nori. They thrive and grow incredibly fast."

All reports are positive and no wonder. Cats and dogs need broad-based mineral support just as we do. They also benefit from chelated, colloidal minerals as opposed to the inorganic salts that leave a free metal ion in the digestive track. They may also be attracted to the highly utilizable protein in most sea veggies. (See "Sea Vegetables and Protein," page 23.) And they probably need those minute quantities of trace minerals just as we do.

Several years ago I watched our tiger cat, Lily, drag a bag of laver out of the kitchen cabinet, rip it open, and devour it. I think she was attracted to the high protein and meaty smell of laver. She also attacked me or my wife when we were eating Sea Chips flavored with kelp or dulse!

Several years ago, my neighbor's dog, Willow, was diagnosed with a severe autoimmune disease called hemolytic anemia. One day at the beach, he dragged in and consumed a large piece of kelp. His owner started sprinkling kelp powder on his food and occasionally fed him cooked whole kelp. He now is completely healed. Could seaweed be part of the reason?

Craig Hoke, MCSV's international marketing manager, has been sprinkling kelp powder and granules on his dog's vegetarian food for years. He has cared for as many as twelve dogs on this regimen and says that both their skin and coats seem to have benefited from the extra seaweed.

Suzanne Birks who developed a seaweed-based dog food for Source Inc. (www.4source.com) has been raising golden Labradors for twenty years. She says her dogs have never developed hip displaisure, hot skin spots, or whelping problems in that period. They also have beautiful coats and good appetites. She recommends 1 tablespoon per 15 pounds of dog per day of their "Source Plus" seaweed-based meal.

Bob Morse, of Atlantic Labs in Waldoboro, Maine, has successfully fed his dogs a seaweed-based meal for years. His company markets an animal feed supplement called "Sea Life" that can be fed to dogs and cats as well as larger animals, horses, goats, or even chickens. See his web page (www.noamkelp.com) for specifics.

Another Maine company, Salt Water Farms started by David and Rebecca Reardon, produces three seaweed-based foods: "Sea Pet" for smaller animals which supposedly helps with their coats, skins, allergies, and hot spots; "Sea Farm" for larger animals which produces more efficient food utilization, improves fertility, and grows better skin and hooves; "Sea Bird" which supposedly improves the ability of eggs to hatch and improves shell texture and strength. Their website is www.saltwaterfarms.com.

All these benefits come from simply sprinkling a little seaweed on your favorite animal's feed daily. You can also bake crunchy treats for your pets with sea veggie pieces or powder as an ingredient in any cracker or flatbread recipe.

Amongst all the good news about feeding seaweed to animals, there is one precaution that Susan Domizi, founder of Source Inc., draws attention to in a paper called "Iodine in the Horse; Too Much or Too Little." In it she sites evidence from horse breeders that excessive iodine in the diet of a brood mare (more than 50 mg per day for a horse eating 10 kg of dry matter) may cause enlarged thyroids or hypothyroidism in their foals. (See "Technical Papers and Articles" on Source Products page at www. 4source.com.) Dogs are evidently not as sensitive to excess iodine as horses, according to Suzanne Birks, Source's dog expert. This is the only possible downside of feeding seaweed to animals that I am aware of.

Growing Plants with Sea Vegetables

Seaweed has been used for centuries as a nutritious fertilizer for all kinds of plants. Coastal farmers in Great Britain and Ireland would lug piles of beached seaweed from the shore back to the furrows of their newly plowed fields. In Brittany wagon loads of seaweed were dragged from the vast intertidal zone at low tide to the fields far inland in France. In North America, coastal Native Americans were known to place fresh seaweed along with fish in their corn and squash hills before planting.

My wife Linnette has been doing something similar for 30 years in her extensive vegetable and flower gardens here in Maine. She will often spread fresh seaweed (mostly rockweed) on the exposed beds in the fall and till them under in the spring. In the summer she often mulches growing plants with some fresh rockweed. But her favorite use for any fresh seaweed is as a crucial ingredient in her massive, layered compost piles. She mixes a light layer of fresh seaweed (or rehydrated scraps from MCSV) with a thin layer of grass clippings, hay, or weeds, then a layer of horse, cow, or chicken manure. Our heavy clay soil has never shown signs of too much sodium, and grows more flavorful, colorful, and nutritious vegetables each year.

Mulching with seaweed is another option. Rockweed is excellent and its sharpness, when dry, is a good slug deterrent. Other seaweeds tend to be slippery and smelly; although covering them with some grass clippings or straw renders them more acceptable to nose and feet. For superior mulch try eelgrass. Though growing in shallow saltwater bays, it is biologically a grass not a seaweed. Its high silica content keeps it from breaking down too fast and smelling as it dries. Linnette covers most open beds with it in the fall, then tills it under in the spring or pulls it aside to plant in the well-protected soil underneath.

One last seaweed solution for houseplants or your garden is called "kelp tea." Simply cover fresh or dried plants with water, leave them at least overnight to steep, then water with the dark brown brew or spray your plants' leaves with it. In addition to other beneficial elements, kelp and rockweed contain cytokinan, a natural growth accelerator that also increases flowering, intensifies color, and increases total yields for your garden.

If you live far from the sea, there are a number of seaweed-based products available in both liquid and dry form. Check with your favorite nursery or agricultural supply store, or go onto the web using key words such as seaweed fertilizer. Several Maine companies already mentioned in this section would be glad to help you. Maine Coast Sea Vegetables sometimes has extra scraps or culls to sell, as does Maine Seaweed Company in Steuben. (See Resources, page 156.) On his North American Kelp site, Bob Morse presents a strong case for using seaweed on just about any plant you are trying to grow. These are some of his claims:

* Increases seed germination and root development;
* Increases bloom set and size of flowers and fruit;
* Relieves stress in plants caused by extreme weather conditions;
* Increases plant resistance to disease, insect attack, drought, and frost;
* Increases microorganisms in the soil that fix nitrogen from the air;
* Increases mineral uptake from the soil;
* Increases storage life of fruits and vegetables by retarding loss of protein, chlorophyll, and RNA.

So whether you are caring for house plants or a truck garden, whether you compost it, spread it, spray it, mulch with it, or till it in, seaweeds' broad spectrum, organic, micronutrients will nourish your plants and the soil, just as they help to nourish your body inside and out.

Caring for Your Skin and Hair with Sea Vegetables

In Japan and other Asian nations, beautiful, healthy hair, skin and nails are attributed to the regular use of sea vegetables in the daily cuisine. Most traditional formulas for shampoo and soap in these countries invariably include at least one sea vegetable ingredient.

What properties of seaweeds are responsible for great hair and nails? That's still under investigation, but it's probably a combination of many factors, such as the abundance of organic colloidal minerals, particularly calcium, silica, iron, and phosphorus; the emulsifying alginates that cleanse surface toxins (they emulsify oils and de-acidify); and the abundance of iodine, amino acids, active enzymes, beta carotene, B vitamins, etc.

We all sense the connection between inner health and outer beauty. Here's a good example from MCSV's "fan mail." Carolyn Neel of Chico, California, writes, "I am 60 years old and began turning gray in my 30th year—mainly around the temple area . . . After I had been using (eating) dulse for at least 6 months, I began to notice darker hair coming in around the temple area and around the neck line. I had been about 90% gray. It is now down to 20% . . . There are a lot of products for the hair that claim wonderful results but I'm staying with dulse flakes."

Here's another story about seaweed and hair from a book about Japanese beauty secrets called *Inner Peace, Outer Beauty*, by Michelle Leigh. "The upper class wives of Samurai used seaweed shampoo, and it was said that this was the source of their strong, shining, beautiful black hair. Seaweed not only removes dirt and excess oil but also improves and imparts a rich supply of nutrients leaving hair lustrous, thick, and easy to arrange. The deep sea aroma can be heady; women of all Japan used so much water to rinse their seaweed-washed heads that public baths charged higher rates for women bathers!"[39]

In her book, Michelle gives a simple recipe for Sea Tangle Shampoo, using 1 teaspoon of powdered dried seaweed to ¾ cup of water. Kelp would be an obvious choice here as it has plentiful alginates that will thicken the shampoo and give your hair great body. If you don't have kelp powder, Michelle suggests blending dried hiziki or kombu into powder. Where fresh seaweed is available, rinse it for 10 to 20 minutes to remove some of the salt, and purée it before adding it to a little water. She recommends preparing the mixture at least 30 minutes before use, probably to allow the alginates to fully hydrate.

When applying this shampoo it may be massaged into the scalp or left for 20 minutes if desired as a "pack." Rinse well at the end, and add a teaspoon of rice vinegar to the final rinse to eliminate organic odors, if there are any.

For those of you not wanting to give up your usual shampoo, Michelle suggests a seaweed tea rinse. This is made by pouring boiling water over a strip of dried kelp or kombu, allowing it to steep for 30 minutes, then removing the kelp before using the warm rinse with a scalp massage.

Now that you have washed and rinsed your hair with seaweed, perhaps you are ready to immerse the rest of your body in a seaweed bath. For that there is no one more enthusiastic than Linda Rector Page, N.D., Ph.D., whose "Healthy Healing" books have turned many folks on to many kinds of natural remedies, including the merits of sea veggies, which she often refers to as "sea greens." No one can say it better, so I will quote her exactly on the subject of bathing and seaweed.

"Seaweed baths are nature's perfect body/psyche balancer. Remember how good you feel after a walk in the ocean? Seaweeds purify ocean pollutants and they can do the same for your body. Rejuvenating effects occur when toxins are released from the body. A hot seaweed bath is like a wet steam sauna only better because the kelps and sea greens balance body chemistry instead of dehydrate it. Electrolytic magnetic action of the seaweed releases excess body fluid from congested cells and dissolves fatty wastes through the skin, replacing them with depleted minerals, particularly potassium and iodine. Iodine boosts thyroid activity, taming the appetite and increasing metabolism so that food fuels are used before they can turn into fatty deposits. Eating sea veggies regularly also has this effect. Vitamin K is another key nutrient in seaweeds. This precursor vitamin helps regulate adrenal function, meaning that a seaweed bath can also help maintain hormone balance for a more youthful body."[40]

To actually take a bath with seaweed, simply choose your favorite dried plant or plants from your pantry and place them in something like a cheesecloth bag whose mesh is fine enough to keep the plants from clogging your drain but loose enough to let the mineral and mucilage into your bath water. Or if you are daring, try a piece of whole kelp, kombu, or alaria without the bag. If you live near the ocean, bring fresh seaweed back (rockweed, kelp, even dulse will work), rinse it thoroughly, and let it loose in your tub. The fresh water will slowly pop the cells, and you will benefit from all that rich intercellular material. You may also notice your water becoming a bit brown from natural dyes and your skin a bit slippery from the mucilaginous material that is released.

Another way to treat your skin to sea veggies is a seaweed body pack. This is a traditional Japanese use that "stimulates, tones, heals, purifies, rejuvenates, and nourishes," according to Michelle in her book on Japanese beauty secrets. She recommends whole wakame but alaria, kelp, or kombu should work equally well. Simply soak the whole dried fronds for 20 minutes to soften. After cleaning your body thoroughly, cover as much of it as possible (or as much as you choose) with the seaweed pieces, and recline for 30 minutes. After removing the seaweed, rinse with cool water. Wow, what a feeling!

There are also numerous soaps, skin creams, and lotions that are formulated with seaweed in them, usually kelp. A customer just notified me of a "Creme De La Mar" at $140.00 per jar in a New York City department store. There is something simpler and cheaper you might try first. Hydrate some agar flakes or kelp powder and add a little to your favorite facial cream or hand lotion. Tina, who works here at Maine Coast Sea Vegetables, actually made a great looking soap with kelp powder, and it was a big hit with our crew. She simply added a few tablespoons of our kelp powder (*Laminaria digitata*) to a basic clear, unscented soap recipe. The result was a misty green bar with a hint of ocean spray! Be creative. Join the long tradition of nourishing skin and hair with seaweed. Celebrate!

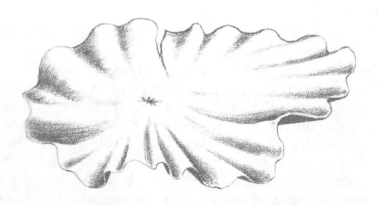

Endnotes

1. *Laminaria digitata* (N. Atlantic) called "sea tangle" in Ireland, "horsetail kelp" in Nova Scotia, "digitata" in America, and "finger tangle" in Europe; *Laminaria saccharina* (N. Atlantic and Pacific) called "sugar wrack" in Western Europe, "hiadui" in China, and "karafuto kombu" in Japan; *Macrocystis pyrifera* (Pacific) called "giant kelp" in America; *Nereocystis lautkeana* (Pacific) called "bull whip kelp" in America; *Aescophyllum nodosum* (N. Atlantic) called "Norwegian kelp" or "rockweed" in Europe and America, and "wrack" in the British Isles; Fucus vesiculosis (N. Atlantic) called "bladderwrack" or "rockweed" in America; *Laminuria japonica* (Pacific) called "Japanese kelp" or "kombu" in America.

2. In domesticating nori, the Japanese uncovered the complex mysteries of this ancient plant's regeneration. The reproductive cycles of most algae involve both an asexual (sporophyte) producing stage and a sexual (gametaphyte) generating stage, where microscopic male and female plants must "mate" to produce the macroplant that in turn will generate more spores. Nori spores, however, first burrow into a seashell to become filamentous conchocelus that produce conchospores that eventually become microscopic nori plants.

3. You may notice little fingers or buds popping out of the sides of your dulse leaf before you pop it in your mouth or as you rinse it in the kitchen. This is another clever reproductive mechanism some seaweeds use to grow called asexual budding, allowing them to propagate even if spore-producing conditions (factors of light, heat, and nutrients) aren't favorable.

4. These include *Laminaria longicruris*, *Laminaria saccharina*, *Laminaria digitata*, and and a type of alaria, *Alaria esculenta*.

In Great Britain, all these species, including *Ascophyllum* and *Fucus*, were collectively known to as kelp (from Middle English "culpe"), which originally referred not to the plants but to the sodium, potassium, and iodine rich ash that was left after burning the plants. The kelp industry in Ireland, Scotland, Norway, and Brittany during the 19th century was substantial. For example, in the early 1800s in Scotland, over 60,000 people made a livelihood from gathering, drying and burning these *Laminarias* in "kelp kilns," selling the salts for use in soap, glass, and iodine manufacturing.

5. Eleanor and John Lewallen, *Sea Vegetable Gourmet Cookbook*, (self published, 1996) 92.

6. V.J. Chapman, *Seaweeds and Their Uses* (London: Methuen & Co., 1950). It is out of print, but try a big library, your local used book dealer, or the internet.

7. Lewallen, *Sea Vegetable Gourmet Cookbook*, 94.

8. Seibin and Teruko Arasaki, *Vegetables From The Sea*, (Tokyo: Japan Publications, 1983) Chapter 1.

9. Eric F.W. Powell, PhD., N.D., *Kelp, The Health Giver* (Essex, England: Health Science Press) 1968, Distributed by Nutri-Books Corp., Denver, Co.

10. Swaha Devi, "Sea Vegetables Are Making A Splash," *Alternative Medicine Magazine* Jan. (2001).

11. Alex Jack, "Let Food Be Thy Medicine," *One Peaceful World Newsletter* 1999, 200.

12. The National Academy of Sciences' Institute of Medicine, latest RDA and UL (upper limit) for iodine, www.nas.edu.

13. Arasaki, *Vegetables From The Sea*, 43.

14. Steven B. Edelson, M.D., "Essential Fatty Acids: The Healing Fats," www.ephca.com.

15. Arasaki, *Vegetables From The Sea*, 44.

16. Arasaki, *Vegetables From The Sea*, Arasaki shows B_{12} results for 5 different Japanese seaweeds with Porphyra (nori) testing at a high range of 13 to 29 micrograms per 100 grams and hijiki and kombu testing less than 1 mcg per 100 grams.

17. The analytical protocol the British chose used a bacteria, Escherienia coli, to isolate the B_{12}. In 1985 Herman Baker et al published a study establishing a protocol using tiny "microanimals" (protozoa, perhaps) called *Ochromonas malhamensis*. They called the method the "Gold Standard" for detecting metabolically active B_{12} "because *O. malhamensis* does not respond to

metabolically inactive B_{12} analogues." They went on to demonstrate why the official USP assay method plus three other methods may show varying degrees of "biologically inactive cobalamines (analogues) which may lead to erroneous assay values." (Baker et al, "Determination of Metabolically Active B_{12} Analog Titers in Human Blood vs Several Microbial Reagents and a Radiodilution Assay" Journal of the American College of Nutrition 5 [1985]: 467-475.) Because of this study, MCSV retested all of its sea veggies for B_{12} using the *Ochromonas malhamensis* method in 1991. In most cases the total B_{12} reported was even greater than the USP method.

18. Some (such as A. Rauma, R. Torronen, et al, "Status of Long-Term Adherents of a Strict Uncooked Vegan Diet" Journal of Nutrition 125 [1995]: 2511-2515), point to the higher levels of serum B_{12} in vegans eating seaweeds while others (Dagnelli et al, "Vitamin B_{12} from Algae Appears not to be Available" American Journal of Clinical Nutrition 53 [1991]: 695-697) observe that the hematological factors failed to improve and that is what counts in turning around B_{12} deficiency.

19. Lewallen, *Sea Vegetable Gourmet Cookbook*, 99.

20. Arasaki, *Vegetables From The Sea*, 35.

21. Swaha Devi, "Sea Vegetables are Making a Splash" *Alternative Medical Journal* (January, 2001).

22. news release of the Biotechnology Research Laboratory of Takara Japan (July 15, 1989).

23. Dr. Zakir Ramazanov, "Marine Source Nutraceuticals," *Nutraceuticals World* 2, no. 6.

24. Arasaki, *Vegetables From The Sea*, 53.

25. Ibid., 38 For more information see the article by Kimura and Kuramoto called, "Influences of Seaweeds on Metabolism of Cholesterol and Anti Coagulant Actions of Seaweed." in the *Tokushima Journal of Experimental Medicine* 21 (1974): 79-88.

26. Arasaki, *Vegetables From The Sea*, 57.

27. Dr. Eric Powell, PhD., N.D., *Kelp, the Health Giver*, 16-17.

28. Deborah Ahern, PhD., RD, "Electrolytic Content of Salt-Replacement Seasonings," *Journal of The American Dietetic Association* 89, no. 7 (1989).

29. "Blood Pressure and Nutrient Intake" *U.S .Science Magazine* 224.

30. Dr. Zakir Ramazanov, "Marine Source Nutraceuticals," *Nutraceuticals World* 2, no. 6.

31. Jane Teas, "The Dietary Intake of Laminaria, a Brown Seaweed, and Breast Cancer Prevention," *Nutrition and Cancer* 4, no. 3 (1983).

32. Dr. Andrew Weil, "Seaweeds: The Wonder Vegetables," *Self Healing Newsletter* (November 1997).

33. S. C. Skoryna et al, "Intestinal Absorption of Radioactive Strontium" *Canadian Medical Association Journal* 191 (1964).

34. Y. Tenaka et al, "Intestinal Absorption of Radioactive Strontium" *Canadian Medical Association Journal* 99 (1968).

35. Steven Schacter, *Fighting Radiation With Food, Herbs and Vitamins*, (Brookline, MA: East West Health Books) 1988.

36. Ibid., 76.

37. Ara Der Marderosian, "Marine Pharmaceuticals," *The Journal of Pharmaceutical Sciences* 58, no.1.

38. Donald R. Davis, Ph.D., *Health Hunter Newsletter* 10, no. 7 (1996).

39. Michelle Dominique Leigh, *Inner Peace, Outer Beauty*, (New York: Carol Publishing Group, Citadel Press) 1992

40. Linda Rector Page, N.D., Ph.D., *Healthy Healing*, (Healthy Healing Publications, 1997)

Appetizers, Spreads, Dips & Snacks

Dulse Olive Tapenade

Yield: 2 to 3 servings

This creative tapenade from Linnette adds a zesty new taste to an old favorite. So versatile, you can serve it on top of spaghetti, pizza, crackers, bread, and even add a dollop to soup.

2 to 3 cloves garlic
One 6-ounce can pitted black olives, drained
1 tablespoon olive oil
⅓ cup **dulse flakes**

Put the garlic cloves, olives, oil, and dulse in the work bowl of a food processor, and purée until smooth. Or you can squeeze the garlic in a press and hand chop the olives until very fine, then stir in the olive oil and dulse.

Per serving: Calories 115, Protein 1 g, Fat 11 g, Carbohydrates 4 g,
Fiber 25 g, Calcium 59 mg, Sodium 536 mg

Hot and Tangy Tapenade
(Olive Spread)

Yield: 1½ cups

This spread from Susan makes pizza come alive. It is wonderful served on crostini, crackers, or as a dip for chips and raw vegetable sticks too.

1 pound kalamata olives
2 tablespoons capers
7 tablespoons **dulse flakes**
2 cloves garlic, peeled and finely chopped
½ teaspoon red pepper flakes, or more to taste
2 tablespoons extra-virgin olive oil
1 tablespoon red wine vinegar

Pit the olives. If the olives and capers are excessively salty, rinse them in several changes of water. Chop the olives and mix them with the capers and the rest of the ingredients. Taste and adjust the seasonings if you like. Add more hot peppers for a spicier taste or more vinegar to cool the heat.

Per 2 tablespoons: Calories 152, Protein 1 g, Fat 16 g, Carbohydrates 4 g,
Fiber 0 g, Calcium 3 mg, Sodium 84 mg

Vegetarian Caviar

Yield: 4 to 6 servings

Inexpensive, simple, and versatile, this caviar is fine with and without champagne. Try serving it on crostini or water biscuits with decorative garnishes or atop baked potatoes with sour cream or fat-free yogurt. Thanks Susan.

10 tablespoons **dulse flakes**
½ cup water
2 tablespoons vegetable oil (mild olive or canola oil)
Finely chopped white onion, chopped egg whites, tiny
    French cornichons (gerkins), lemon wedges for garnish
    (optional)

Mix the dulse, water, and oil together. Let the mixture marinate in a closed jar in the refrigerator with any of the optional garnishes for 24 hours before serving.

Per serving: Calories 56, Protein 1 g, Fat 5 g, Carbohydrates 1 g,
Fiber 1 g, Calcium 6 mg, Sodium 46 mg

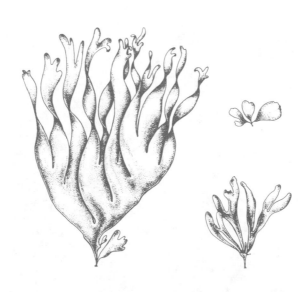

Nutty Bean Spread

Yield: 4 to 6 servings

Like a French pâté, you can serve this on crackers or bread. It is also a lovely sandwich filling with greens.

1½ cup lentils, rinsed
½ cup walnuts
One 1- to 5-inch piece of **kelp**
3 cups water
2½ tablespoons miso
½ cup chopped parsley
2 to 3 cloves garlic, minced

Simmer the lentils, walnuts, and kelp in the water for 45 minutes to an hour until the water is absorbed and the lentils are soft. Mash the lentils and walnuts with the miso, parsley, and garlic. Taste and adjust the seasonings. Chill and serve.

Per serving: Calories 263, Protein 16 g, Fat 9 g, Carbohydrates 34 g, Fiber 13 g, Calcium 64 mg, Sodium 369 mg

❖ *Try other bean and nut combinations: split peas and cashews; aduki beans and almonds; or yellow split peas and sunflower or pumpkin seeds.*

Black Bean-Sunflower Spread/ Dressing/Dip/Soup

Yield: 2 to 4 servings

Wendy whipped up the following goodies as a spread. Add more water and/or lemon juice to change the consistency toward soup.

- 2 tablespoons lemon juice
- 2 tablespoons water or soup stock
- ½ cup cooked black turtle beans
- ½ cup hulled sunflower seeds
- 1 teaspoon ginger
- ¼ teaspoon garlic powder
- ¾ teaspoon **dulse granules**
- ½ teaspoon **kelp granules**
- ¼ teaspoon **nori granules** (optional)
- Chopped parsley or scallions, for garnish (optional)

Blend all the ingredients, except the garnish, in a bowl or blender.

Per serving: Calories 185, Protein 8 g, Fat 13 g, Carbohydrates 12 g, Fiber 5 g, Calcium 39 mg, Sodium 6 mg

Smoked Dulse Carrot Spread

Yield: 4 servings

Stuff this tuna-tasting spread into pita for a fabulous lunch or snack. You can also serve it on greens or crackers, or use as a sandwich spread.

1 cup carrot pulp or grated carrot
⅓ cup chopped **smoked dulse**
4 teaspoons **nori granules**
2 teaspoons minced onion
2 teaspoons minced celery
⅛ teaspoon grated ginger
½ teaspoon lemon juice
⅓ to ½ cup soy mayonnaise

Mix all the ingredients together, adding the mayonnaise last. Taste and adjust the seasonings, if desired.

Per serving: Calories 127, Protein 1 g, Fat 11 g, Carbohydrates 7 g, Fiber 1 g, Calcium 13 mg, Sodium 121 mg

Cucumber Kelp Pickles

Yield: 6 to 8 servings

Kelp goes well in just about every pickle recipe. This is a very simple one from Sharon Rhoads that utilizes the natural salts in kelp and fermented soy.

12 inches dried **kelp**
1 medium cucumber
¼ cup soy sauce

Lightly rinse the kelp and cut into 2-inch x ½-inch strips. Wash the cucumber thoroughly, and cut into thick rounds. Place the kelp strips in a sterilized crock or pickle jar. Pour in the soy sauce, then mix in the cucumber rounds. Cover and refrigerate at least 24 hours.

Replenish the ingredients as they are used. The pickling mixture can be used three to four times.

Per serving: Calories 17, Protein 2 g, Fat 0 g, Carbohydrates 2 g, Fiber 1 g, Calcium 20 mg, Sodium 145 mg

Dulse Oyster Sauce

Yield: ¾ cup (7 to 8 servings)

This vegetarian version of a Chinese oyster sauce is lower in sodium, but tastes like the real thing. Besides, most commercial oyster sauces contain artificial and imitation oyster flavoring, caramel coloring, and other unauthentic ingredients. You deserve the best! Feel free to use the ingredients of this recipe as the model for your own recipe. Thanks Susan.

7 tablespoons **dulse flakes**
Water to cover
¼ cup white wine
1 teaspoon sugar

Put the dulse flakes in a 1-pint measuring cup. Add enough water to cover. Let settle for 10 minutes, then strain through a chinois or with cheesecloth, pressing down to extract as much essence as possible. Add the wine and sugar to the resulting liquid, and store in the refrigerator. Reduce over medium heat for a more concentrated sauce.

Per serving: Calories 21, Protein 1 g, Fat 0 g, Carbohydrates 3 g, Fiber 0 g, Calcium 12 mg, Sodium 87 mg

❖ *If you want to add dulse to commercial oyster sauce, add 7 table-spoons of **dulse flakes** and about ¼ cup white wine to every 2 teaspoons oyster sauce called for in any recipe.*

Dulse Cocktail Sauce

Yield: 10 servings (3 tablespoons)

This cocktail sauce was developed by Eleanor to carry the built-in flavor of the sea.

1 cup natural-style catsup
¼ cup prepared horseradish
½ cup lemon juice
2 tablespoons **dulse flakes**
1 teaspoon sea salt
1 tablespoon maple syrup

Combine all the ingredients and let stand for 15 minutes to allow the flavors to come together.

Per serving: Calories 38, Protein 1 g, Fat 0 g, Carbohydrates 10 g, Fiber 1 g, Calcium 13 mg, Sodium 521 mg

Laver Condiment

Yield: about 2 cups (8 to 10 servings)

Here's a simple and extremely tasty condiment made with wild laver. It comes from an East-West Foundation cooking class in Boston. A little of bit of this ocean goddess goes a long way. Use the recipe as a guide, and adjust the quantities to suit your taste. Serve a little with grains and veggies, or use it to flavor a spread, soup, or salad dressing.

1 cup **laver**, soaked until limp, and chopped
½ cup soy sauce
½ cup water
3 drops mirin (optional)

Cover the chopped laver in a saucepan with the soy sauce and water. Simmer covered until all the liquid is absorbed or evaporated (approximately 1 to 1½ hours). Check occasionally. Be careful not to burn. Add a few drops of mirin to enrich the flavor. Store in the refrigerator in a covered jar. This will last for several weeks.

Per serving: Calories 10, Protein 2 g, Fat 0 g, Carbohydrates 1 g, Fiber 0 g, Calcium 5 mg, Sodium 894 mg

Heavenly House Spice Mix

Yield: about ½ cup

Place this in small glass dishes on your table instead of salt and pepper. Thanks Susan.

4 tablespoons **dulse granules**
1 tablespoon cumin seeds, coarsely ground
1 tablespoon fennel seeds, coarsely ground
1 tablespoon sesame seeds, coarsely ground
½ tablespoon white peppercorns, coarsely ground
¼ tablespoon cayenne

Mix all the ingredients. Store in a tightly closed container.

Per teaspoon: Calories 6, Protein 0 g, Fat 0 g, Carbohydrates 1 g, Fiber 0 g, Calcium 11 mg, Sodium 15 mg

❖ *Mix with extra-virgin olive oil or unrefined walnut oil. This is heavenly when spread on toasted French bread with a meal or served as an appetizer.*

Alaria Condiment

Yield: about ¾ cup

*This is another idea from Sharon Rhoads that goes well with just about any-
thing: grains, veggies, chips, crackers, salads, sandwiches, etc. It also saves
you time. Cooking alaria from scratch is a lengthy process, but here it is a
ready-to-use condiment to keep in the refrigerator like mustard or ketchup.*

- 1 cup tightly packed **alaria** (1 ounce)
- 1 medium onion, chopped
- 1 tablespoon sesame oil or your preferred oil
- 1 teaspoon soy sauce
- 1 teaspoon miso
- 1 teaspoon sake (optional)

Cover the alaria with water, and soak for 10 minutes. Drain and
reserve the soaking water. Slice the alaria into small pieces by
lining up the midribs.

Discard any shells you might find in the reserved water. Put the
alaria in a pressure cooker with 1 cup of reserved soaking water,
bring up to pressure, and cook for 25 minutes. Let it cool, then
drain. If you do not have a pressure cooker, simmer the alaria in
2 cups of water for 30 to 45 minutes until tender.

Sauté the onion in the oil until golden, stirring and adding a bit
of water if necessary. Add the alaria and cook another minute,
stirring. Put the mixture in a bowl or jar, and add the soy sauce,
miso, and sake, stirring well. Refrigerate several hours or
overnight before serving.

Per 1½ tablespoons: Calories 28, Protein 1 g, Fat 2 g, Carbohydrates 3 g,
Fiber 1 g, Calcium 30 mg, Sodium 161 mg

Dulse Snacks

(especially for kids)

Dulse Chips: Fry small pieces of dry dulse in a liberally oiled pan until the leaves turn dark green and crisp.

Dulse Sandwiches: Add some dulse chips or soaked raw dulse to any sandwich. Add some cooked beans for a DBLT.

Dulse OTB: Watch out. Eating dulse right Out of The Bag is addictive. If a child likes dulse at all, this could become his/her "bag."

Dulse Plugs: a teenager's revenge, and a tobacco alternative still used in the Maritime Provinces. Wad up a few dulse leaves in your palm and pop into the cheek. Guaranteed to shock others but not your nervous system.

Alaria Chips

Yield: 4 to 6 servings

Here's a sure fire-way to introduce alaria to kids. The midribs can be a bit chewy, so cut them out if you want these chips to melt in your mouth.

1 to 2 feet of quickly rinsed **alaria**
1 to 2 tablespoons sesame oil

Chop the rinsed alaria into bite-size pieces. Heat the oil in a heavy skillet over medium heat.

Press pieces of alaria into the hot oil until they turn green and become crisp. Drain them on paper towels, and allow them to cool, but don't wait too long to serve them or they'll lose their crackle.

Per serving: Calories 55, Protein 1 g, Fat 4 g, Carbohydrates 3 g,
Fiber 3 g, Calcium 78 mg, Sodium 299 mg

Smoky Nachos

Yield: 6 to 8 servings

For the kid in all of us.

> 6 ounces Maine Coast Sea Chips or nacho chips
> 1 cup salsa
> 2 cups grated soy, cheddar, or Monterey Jack cheese
> 1½ cups chopped, loosely packed **smoked dulse**
> **Dulse/Garlic Sea Seasonings** to taste

Layer the chips onto a baking pan, and sprinkle with the salsa, grated cheese, smoked dulse, and Dulse/Garlic Sea Seasonings. Broil for 5 to 10 minutes. Serve hot.

Per serving: Calories 217, Protein 10 g, Fat 12 g, Carbohydrates 20 g, Fiber 2 g, Calcium 90 mg, Sodium 613 mg

Toasted Laver & Pumpkin Seeds

Yield: 1 to 4 servings

Low-fat, high in minerals, and vitamins! Try it as a snack or garnish for grains.

> 1 cup chopped **laver**
> ½ cup pumpkin seeds
> 1 teaspoon soy sauce (optional)

Preheat the oven to 300°F. Toast the laver for 5 to 8 minutes until crisp, or dry roast it in a medium skillet, turning occasionally until crisp and green. Set aside in a bowl.

In a frying pan, roast the pumpkin seeds over medium heat, stirring frequently until they pop and turn golden. Combine the toasted laver and pumpkin seeds in a bowl, and set aside to cool.

Per serving: Calories 165, Protein 9 g, Fat 12 g, Carbohydrates 7 g, Fiber 6 g, Calcium 11 mg, Sodium 19 mg

❖ *If desired, add soy sauce to the pumpkin seeds, and stir while cooking.*

Sea Palm Tempura

Yield: 6 servings

Serve this with grated daikon radish atop a bowl of soba noodles in a ginger tamari broth, or alone with radish and dip sauce.

½ ounce **sea palm fronds**
¼ cup brown rice flour
¼ cup whole wheat pastry flour
1 heaping teaspoon arrowroot plus enough for "dusting"
Pinch of sea salt
½ to ⅔ cup cold water
Oil for frying (sunflower, safflower, or soy)
Grated daikon radish

Rinse and soak the palm fronds in water for ½ hour. Meanwhile mix the flours, arrowroot, and sea salt, and stir in the cold water. Drain the palm fronds and blot dry on a cotton towel. Dust with the additional arrowroot, mixing well.

In a deep kettle or saucepan, heat the oil to abut 365°F. Do not fill the kettle more than half full with oil. You will need room for the battered food and for the bubbling of the oil. When the oil is hot enough, a little batter dropped into it should rise at once to the surface. Dip a small bunch of fronds in the batter, drain for 5 seconds, and drop in the oil to fry until golden on each side. Do not crowd the pan.

Drain the fronds on a paper towel, and place them in a warm oven to stay crisp until eaten. Repeat with the next bunch of palm fronds, raising and lowering the flame so as not to burn the oil but cook the sea palm fronds quickly. Never reuse frying oil.

Per serving: Calories 52, Protein 2 g, Fat 0 g, Carbohydrates 10 g, Fiber 2 g, Calcium 27 mg, Sodium 101 mg

Sea Vegetable Tempura

Yield: 4 to 6 servings

Kids tend to like fried foods, in case you haven't noticed! Here's a relatively nutritious alternative you might slip by someone who's not sure about eating seaweed to begin with.

¼ to ½ ounce **dulse** and/or **kelp**
¼ cup brown rice flour
¼ cup whole wheat pastry flour
1 heaping teaspoon arrowroot flour plus enough for "dusting"
Pinch of sea salt
½ to ⅔ cup cold water
Oil for frying (sunflower, safflower, or soy)

Soak the dulse for 1 minute or the kelp for 20 minutes. Cut the kelp into bite-size pieces; bunch the dulse into little balls.

Mix the flours, arrowroot, and sea salt, and stir in the cold water.

In a deep kettle or saucepan, heat the oil to abut 365°F. Do not fill the kettle more than half full with oil. You will need room for the battered food and for the bubbling of the oil. When the oil is hot enough, a little batter dropped into the oil should rise at once to the surface. Dip some of the dulse or kelp in the batter, drain for 5 seconds, and drop in the oil to fry until golden on each side. Do not crowd the pan.

Drain on a paper towel, and place them in a warm oven to stay crisp until eaten. Repeat with the next bunch, raising and lowering the flame so as not to burn the oil but cook them quickly. Never reuse frying oil.

Don't let little hands grab one of these for a few minutes. They are hot!

Per serving: Calories 59, Protein 2 g, Fat 0 g, Carbohydrates 12 g, Fiber 2 g, Calcium 5 mg, Sodium 33 mg

Avocado Dulse Dip

Yield: 2 servings

1 tablespoon **dulse flakes** or **granules**
1 avocado, chopped
3 scallions, diced
1 tablespoon lemon juice
⅛ teaspoon cayenne

Blend all the ingredients and serve with sprouted bread or with carrots, celery, broccoli, etc.

Per serving: Calories 177, Protein 3 g, Fat 15 g, Carbohydrates 11 g, Fiber 65 g, Calcium 32 mg, Sodium 57 mg

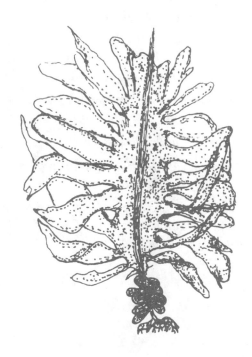

Sea Salsa Verde

Yield: 1½ cups

Great on potatoes, pasta, or lavishly spread on dark bread, this salsa keeps 4 to 5 days in the refrigerator, or longer if frozen. Thanks Susan.

- 1 cup tightly packed **laver** (1 ounce)
- ¾ pound tomatillos (about 15)
- 1 to 2 tablespoons chopped fresh jalapeño peppers (red if possible)
- ½ medium red onion, chopped
- 1 teaspoon ground cumin, or to taste
- 3 tablespoons fresh lime juice
- 4 cloves garlic, coarsely chopped

Preheat the oven to 300°F. Toast the laver for 5 to 8 minutes until crisp, or dry roast it in a medium skillet, turning occasionally until crisp. Lightly rinse the toasted laver.

Remove the papery husk from the tomatillos, and steam them with the laver until soft. Blend until smooth in a food processor or blender. Mix in the remaining ingredients.

Per ¼ cup: Calories 49, Protein 3 g, Fat 1 g, Carbohydrates 8 g, Fiber 4 g, Calcium 15 mg, Sodium 165 mg

Quick & Easy

*Simply add **Kelp Granules Sea Seasonings** to taste to your favorite salsa.*

*Add **Kelp with Cayenne** for extra zing! Serve with corn chips or Maine Coast Sea Chips, (organic corn chips flavored with dulse and garlic), crackers, bread sticks, or vegetable sticks.*

Sea Seasonings

Kelp/Cayenne Salsa

Yield: 6 to 8 servings

Make your own salsa from scratch with this easy recipe.

2 cups chopped, ripe tomatoes, or one 16-ounce can plum tomatoes, chopped
½ cup chopped onion
1 teaspoon dried cilantro
⅛ cup vinegar
1 tablespoon chopped jalapeños
4 teaspoons **Kelp/Cayenne Sea Seasonings**, or 2 teaspoons **Kelp/Cayenne** and 2 teaspoons **Dulse/Garlic Sea Seasonings**

Put all the ingredients in a large mixing bowl, and mix well. Taste and adjust the seasonings, if desired.

Per serving: Calories 19, Protein 1 g, Fat 0 g, Carbohydrates 4 g, Fiber 1 g, Calcium 15 mg, Sodium 128 mg

Using Sprinkles

With Maine Coast Sea Vegetables Sea Seasonings, you can enhance the flavor and nutrition of salsa, dressings, dips, popcorn, and more.

Dulse/Garlic Bread

Spread liberal amounts of butter on regular or French bread slices. Sprinkle on *Dulse/Garlic Sea Seasonings* until the butter is lightly covered. Place under a broiler or in a toaster oven for a few minutes. Olive or sesame oil may be substituted for butter.

Dulse/Garlic Popcorn

Toss freshly popped corn with melted butter or dark (roasted) sesame oil. Sprinkle on *Dulse/Garlic Sea Seasonings* liberally, and toss again. *Nori/Ginger Sea Seasonings* also tastes great on popcorn.

Kelp/Cayenne Guacamole

Yield: ½ cup

Kelp and cayenne granules make tasty guacamole. You can also shake kelp granules on boiled eggs or mash them into egg salad.

1 ripe avocado
4 teaspoons lemon juice
4 teaspoons **Kelp/Cayenne Sea Seasonings**
¼ onion, diced (optional)

Peel and mash the avocado with a fork or in a blender. Add the rest of the ingredients, and mix together.

Per tablespoon: Calories 44, Protein 1 g, Fat 3 g, Carbohydrates 4 g, Fiber 1 g, Calcium 6 mg, Sodium 12 mg

Dulse/Garlic Dip

Yield: 6 to 8 servings

1 cup water
½ cup sesame tahini
1 to 3 teaspoons **Dulse/Garlic Sea Seasonings**
Lemon juice or vinegar (optional)

Slowly stir the water into the tahini until the mixture becomes creamy and white. Add Dulse/Garlic Sea Seasonings to taste. Add more water for a delicious sauce or even more water plus lemon juice or vinegar for a tasty salad dressing.

Per serving: Calories 99, Protein 3 g, Fat 8 g, Carbohydrates 5 g, Fiber 2 g, Calcium 73 mg, Sodium 21 mg

Quick & Easy

Low-Fat Deep Sea Dip

*Add diced scallions and **Dulse Granules Sea Seasonings** or **Dulse/Garlic Sea Seasonings** to low-fat sour cream or tofu dip. Use a little or a lot, however you prefer. Serve with celery and carrot sticks, red bell pepper slices, etc.*

BREAKFAST

Flax Date Nut Cereal

Yield: about 5 cups (6 to 8 servings)

Adding toasted laver to granola is outrageously good and a bit exotic. You can also add nori sprinkles to your favorite store-bought granola.

⅔ cup **laver**
1 cup flaxseeds
2 cups rolled oats
½ to ¾ cup dates or raisins
½ cup chopped almonds
2 teaspoons cinnamon
⅔ cup rice syrup
1 teaspoon vanilla
1 teaspoon to 1 tablespoon canola or corn oil

Preheat the oven to 300ºF. Toast the laver for 5 to 8 minutes until crisp, or dry roast it in a medium skillet, turning occasionally until crisp. Crumble the toasted laver into a large mixing bowl.

Grind ¾ cup of the flaxseeds in a blender. Add it to the laver with the remaining ¼ cup whole flaxseeds, the rolled oats, dates, almonds, and cinnamon.

In a small pot, gently boil the rice syrup for 1 minute, and add the vanilla. Mix the syrup and vanilla into the dry mix. Taste and adjust the seasonings, if desired.

Lightly oil a cookie sheet, and evenly spread the granola mix on it. Increase the oven temperature to 350ºF, and bake for 15 minutes, stirring every 5 minutes.

Per serving: Calories 411, Protein 11 g, Fat 16 g, Carbohydrates 63 g,
Fiber 10 g, Calcium 109 mg, Sodium 9 mg

Snack Granola

Yield: 4 to 6 servings

Chris Madden from Philadelphia gave us this recipe. He says, "This is one of the most delicious and yet healthful things to munch I've ever found. It saved my sanity when I quit smoking!"

⅓ cup each: (all or any combination depending on
   preferences; amounts may also be varied)
Puffed millet or other puffed cereal
Rolled quinoa
Rolled oats
Rolled barley
Rolled wheat
Rolled rye
Sesame seeds
Sunflower seeds
Chopped pumpkin seeds
Chopped pecans
Chopped walnuts
Chopped almonds
Roasted and crumbled **kelp**
¼ cup maple syrup and/or barley malt or rice syrup) thinned
   with a little water

Thoroughly mix the dry ingredients with the sweetener until they are all moistened. Spread on a cookie sheet, and bake at low heat (250°F to 300°F) for about 40 minutes, stirring at least once during baking so everything gets evenly toasted. Once it is cool, you can eat it by the handful and enjoy a slightly sweet, salty treat!

Per serving: Calories 499, Protein 16 g, Fat 30 g, Carbohydrates 48 g,
Fiber 10 g, Calcium 178 mg, Sodium 73 mg

❖ *You can also try adding coconut, poppy seeds, black walnuts, soy nuts, etc.*

Nori-Onion Omelet

Yield: 3 to 4 servings

For those who love eggs and onions, this dish is for you. Double the recipe and it becomes a main dish, or makes enough for tomorrow's lunch. Thanks Eleanor.

½ cup **laver**
1 medium onion, diced
5 cloves garlic, thinly sliced
5 eggs
2 tablespoons canola or extra-virgin olive oil
1 tablespoon light yellow or white miso (optional)
2 tablespoons mayonnaise (optional)
Parsley or alfalfa sprouts for garnish
Soy sauce (optional)

Preheat the oven to 300ºF. Toast the laver for 5 to 8 minutes until crisp, or dry roast it in a medium skillet, turning occasionally until crisp. Crumble into flakes and sauté with the onion and garlic in 1 tablespoon of the oil until the onions are translucent. Turn off the heat.

Scramble the eggs in a bowl. Mix in the sautéed onions and garlic. Heat the frying pan and add the remaining tablespoon of oil. Add the egg and onion mixture, and cook on low heat. (Before attempting to flip the omelet, you may want to cut it in half or quarters and flip each section separately.)

If you want to make a spread, mix the miso and mayonnaise together while the omelet is frying.

Garnish with parsley, sprouts, and/or roasted nori, and serve.

If you have any left over, it is delicious in sandwiches or spread on crackers.

❖ *Add some sliced mushrooms and/or ½ cup diced celery.*

❖ *Instead of making an omelet, you can make scrambled eggs.*

❖ *You can use salsa, miso only, or another favorite topping in place of the mayonnaise mix.*

Per serving: Calories 177, Protein 9 g, Fat 13 g, Carbohydrates 6 g, Fiber 1 g, Calcium 47 mg, Sodium 82 mg

Bouillabaisse de Legumes (page 78) pictured to the right.

Tofu Scramble

Yield: 4 servings

Tasty dulse is simple to add to a sauté any time of day.

- 1 tablespoon extra-virgin olive oil or canola oil
- 4 to 6 scallions, chopped, green parts reserved, or
  1 small onion, chopped
- 6 to 8 medium mushrooms, sliced
- 1 pound firm or extra-firm tofu, well drained
- ½ teaspoon turmeric for yellow "scrambled egg" color
  (optional)
- 5 heaping teaspoons nutritional yeast flakes
- 2 tablespoons **dulse flakes**
- 6 to 8 parsley sprigs, diced
- 1 teaspoon tamari
- Sprinkle of black pepper
- Red or yellow bell pepper, thinly sliced (for garnish)

Heat a skillet and add the oil. Sauté the white parts of the scallions 3 to 5 minutes until transparent. Add the mushrooms and sauté another 2 minutes.

Mash or crumble the tofu. Add it to the pan with the turmeric. Sauté until hot and steaming. Mix in the nutritional yeast, dulse, scallion greens, parsley, and tamari. Sprinkle in black pepper. Taste and adjust the seasonings. Garnish with the bell pepper slices.

Per serving: Calories 250, Protein 23 g, Fat 14 g, Carbohydrates 13 g,
Fiber 4 g, Calcium 281 mg, Sodium 161 mg

Mediterranean Salad with Dulse (page 97) pictured to the left.

Nori/Ginger Tofu Scramble

Yield: 4 servings

1 pound fresh tofu
2 tablespoons nutritional yeast flakes
2 tablespoons **Nori/ Ginger Sea Seasonings**

Crumble the tofu into a lightly oiled skillet, and mash with a fork. Simmer for a few minutes, and add a small amount of water for a softer texture, if you wish. Stir in the nutritional yeast flakes and Nori/Ginger Sea Seasonings. You can also add a dash of soy sauce and/or sprinkle on some roasted sesame seeds.

Per serving: Calories 207, Protein 22 g, Fat 10 g, Carbohydrates 9 g,
Fiber 6 g, Calcium 241 mg, Sodium 36 mg

SOUPS

Sea Vegetables in Soup

Many different sea vegetables can be used to make soup. In fact, simmering a sea vegetable in water makes a tasty soup stock without a fuss. It adds minerals to the pot too. How much should you use? It depends on whether you would like to use sea veggies as herbs or major ingredients. Either way you win.

To make a soup, simply simmer or pressure cook sea vegetables in water or stock. Add one or more spices like ginger or bay leaves to enhance digestion and give an ethnic flair. You can use one sea vegetable or a combination to enhance the flavor of your soup. Feel free to garnish soups with dulse flakes or thin strips of toasted nori.

Any of these sea vegetables—dulse, arame, sea palm, alaria, wakame, kelp, and kombu—can be simmered, sautéed, or pressure cooked to make a delicious soup or stock. You can't go wrong with any of them. In fact, I love having many of them on hand so I can always pick and choose the one that suits my mood and schedule. For the times when I need to make a quick soup, I choose between dulse and arame. In the mood for a soft wide noodle? Sea palm is the one that easily pleases the kids and everyone else. Making a fancy French onion soup with herb croutons? Alaria or wakame is a nutritious choice. When I think of cooking bean soups, kelp comes to mind, especially when I have lots of time to cook from scratch. Since all the sea vegetables are loaded with minerals and are so easy to cook with, I hardly make a soup without one.

Making Soup Stock with Sea Vegetables

As a minimum, I recommend using at least a 3- to 5-inch strip of dulse, alaria, wakame, kelp, digitata, or kombu per quart of water. A handful or about ⅛ cup of arame or sea palm is delicious too. You can add more to suit your taste.

If you are thinking about boosting your mineral content, use your imagination and add one or two different sea vegetables from the start. Think of sea vegetables as a perfect substitute for table salt or other additional salty seasonings. Taste the soup before adding salt. You may be surprised by how little salt you will need to balance the flavors.

Dulse: For a quick soup, choose dulse. It is fast and flavorful. Simply add a 3- to 5-inch long piece or several strips, ¼ to ⅓ cup per serving, if you desire a rich seafood taste. Dulse is a super choice for tomato, potato, or grain soups such as chowder, minestrone, and bouillabaisse. If you choose dulse for a long-simmering bean soup, it will dissolve.

Quick Asian Soup—Add a strip of dulse to water, bring to a boil, and simmer for 5 minutes or less until the dulse turns a lighter color. Then add one or more seasonal greens, such as bok choy, Chinese cabbage, spinach, tat soi, mizuna, collard greens, or watercress. As they enter the steaming pot, the vegetables will turn bright green. Turn off the heat and add the final seasonings. Stir in a little miso or tamari, grated ginger, or drizzle on toasted sesame or hot pepper oil. Garnish with fresh chopped scallions, if you like. For a quick meal, add some cooked noodles and cubed tofu.

Arame: Mildly sweet, black, and thin with a noodle-like texture, arame is a natural choice for a quick, Asian-style soup. Imported from Japan, it pairs well with ginger, noodles, tofu, greens, and root vegetables, and is ready in 5 minutes.

Alaria and **Wakame** can be used interchangeably. Both are mild in flavor with a soft texture and delicate green color once they are cooked. These two vegetables compliment most grain, bean, or broth-based soups. To make a fabulous onion soup, simply simmer lots of onions in twice as much water, a bay leaf or two, and lots of alaria or wakame for 1 to 2 hours. The longer it simmers, the sweeter the soup will be. Season to taste with miso, sea salt, and pepper, or tamari. Alaria and wakame are the classic seaweeds for miso soup.

Alaria has a central midrib. To reduce cooking time (usually 45 minutes), cut out the midrib. Simmer 20 minutes like wakame. If you are in a hurry, pressure cook wakame or alaria for 5 to 6 minutes. Presoaking for 1 to 12 hours or pre-roasting for 3 minutes at 300ºF will also reduce the usual cooking time by 5 to 10 minutes.

Kelp, (*L. longicruris*), digitata (*L. digitata*), and kombu (*L. Japonica*) replace beef and chicken stocks. Simmer a 5-inch strip per quart of water or soup stock for at least 10 minutes, then remove if desired. Leave it in the soup longer for a richer flavor. If you like, you can remove the kelp, chop it up, and put it back into the soup pot. With hours of cooking, kelp will dissolve. Kombu and digitata remain tough, more like lasagne noodles, but flavor the soup just fine. Since these are long-cooking sea veggies, they are great for cooking beans from scratch and making long-simmering bean soups such as curried split pea, Mexican chili bean, or Brazilian black bean.

Sea Palm is the fettuccini of sea vegetables and is a wonderful substitute for noodles in soups. Try it in minestrone or other Italian-inspired soups. Sea palm is a children's favorite in miso shiitake vegetable soups. Thai-spicy soups are also wonderful with sea palm.

Advantages to presoaking sea vegetables

I like to simply cut up dried sea vegetables and add them to the soup pot, but you can presoak sea vegetables for anywhere between 1 minute to overnight, if you like.

The longer you presoak sea vegetables, the shorter the cooking time. The longer the soak, the more minerals dissolve into the soaking water, which you add to the soup like a rich soup stock. If you do not add the soaking water, your soup will taste less salty and may need more miso or other seasonings.

How to presoak sea vegetables

Simply put them in a bowl or mug, cover them with water, and let them soak. Ten to 15 minutes of presoaking is long enough to soften seaweeds so that you can easily chop them up like a bunch of greens before simmering them.

Miso

There are many kinds of miso available—mellow, aged 6 months to 1 year (aduki, chick-pea, rice, barley) and white misos are less salty than the 3-year barley, dandelion leek, hatcho, and mugi misos. In any case, choose a flavor that suits your palate and needs, or stock a couple of flavors, such as a 3-year barley miso and a lighter one like chick-pea miso.

Instant Soup Stock

For each pint of water, stir in 2 to 3 teaspoons **dulse flakes** for a mildly salty flavor without overpowering other flavors. Add a bit more dulse, to taste, if using in a strongly seasoned recipe. With long cooking, dulse will dissolve.

For a quick consommé-like soup, simply strain the dulse flakes out, and you will have mineral-rich, subtly sweet, relatively low-sodium stock for soup.

Basic Sea Vegetable Broth

Yield: 6 cups (4 to 6 servings as an appetizer)

Kelp makes great soup stock. Its abundant minerals and "natural MSG" imparts richness to soup usually associated with chicken, beef, or fish.

- 4 to 5 cups water
- 4- to 5-inch strip **kelp** or **kombu**
- ⅓ cup dried shiitake or other mushrooms
- 1 teaspoon minced fresh ginger
- 1 tablespoon miso
- 3 scallions, chopped, for garnish

Bring the water to a boil in a 2-quart soup pot. Add the kelp and dried mushrooms, and let them simmer for 1 hour. Remove the sea vegetable and mushrooms, dice, and return them to the pot. Add the ginger and simmer for 15 minutes. Stir in the miso and garnish with the scallions. Serve as is or use as stock.

Per serving: Calories 23, Protein 1 g, Fat 0 g, Carbohydrates 5 g, Fiber 1 g, Calcium 22 mg, Sodium 190 mg

Rice Tomato Soup

Yield: 4 servings

Juicy tomatoes, aromatic thyme, and bay leaves team up with alaria and rice for a full-bodied soup that is as delightful as an ocean breeze.

1 large onion, chopped
1 tablespoon olive oil
2 large carrots or 3 to 4 small carrots, sliced
⅔ cup **alaria**, snipped in small pieces
1 cup brown rice, rinsed
3 cups water
One 32-ounce can chopped tomatoes, or about 6 to 8 large
   fresh tomatoes, chopped
2 teaspoons thyme
1 bay leaf
Salt and pepper to taste
1 bunch parsley, for garnish

Sauté the onion in the oil for 2 to 3 minutes in a medium saucepan or skillet. Add the carrots and sauté a few minutes until the carrots turn bright orange. Add the remaining ingredients, except the parsley. Simmer over low heat for 45 minutes until the rice and vegetables are tender.

Remove from the heat and garnish with the fresh parsley.

Per serving: Calories 255, Protein 7 g, Fat 5 g, Carbohydrates 47 g,
Fiber 8 g, Calcium 130 mg, Sodium 541 mg

❖ *Substitute wild rice, basmati, or jasmine rice for some or all of the brown rice.*

Creamy Carrot Soup

Yield: 6 to 8 servings

Hearty and warming, this is a soothing soup for a cool autumn day. Thanks Linnette.

- 1- to 5-inch strip **kelp**
- 4 cups water
- 5 medium carrots, chopped
- 3 small to medium potatoes, chopped
- 2 large leeks, chopped (don't use much of the green part), or 2 to 3 medium onions, chopped
- 2 cups soymilk
- 4 tablespoons tamari
- Black pepper and tarragon to taste

Put the kelp and water in a soup pot, and bring to a boil. Add the carrots, potatoes, and leeks, and simmer until tender, about 15 to 20 minutes. Or pressure cook 3 to 4 minutes.

Put half the soup, 1 cup soymilk, 2 tablespoons tamari, black pepper, and tarragon in a blender, and process until smooth. Repeat with the other half of the ingredients.

For a beautiful orange soup, remove the kelp before blending. Most of the nutrients will have already dissolved into the water. For a greener soup with all the sea vegetable's nutrients, blend with the kelp.

Per serving: Calories 127, Protein 5 g, Fat 2 g, Carbohydrates 24 g, Fiber 5 g, Calcium 53 mg, Sodium 655 mg

Basic Miso Soup with Alaria

Yield: 2 to 4 servings

Thanks to Linnette, this is the soup that got Maine Coast Sea Vegetables started in 1971. For over a thousand years, traditional Japanese farmers and fishermen had a bowl of miso sea vegetable soup every morning. Their cultivated wakame looks and tastes very similar to Maine's wild alaria. Because alaria has a midrib, it needs to be cooked longer than wakame. If you are in a hurry, cut out the midrib, or use a quicker cooking sea vegetable, such as wakame, dulse, kelp, or sea palm. See the tips on soaking (page 7) and miso (page 75).

One 12-inch section **alaria,** soaked
1 medium onion, sliced or diced
1 teaspoon sesame oil
4 cups water
Scallions or chives, chopped, for garnish
1½ to 2½ teaspoons hacho or mugi miso

Soak the alaria for 10 minutes. Chop it into bite-size pieces, and sauté with the onion in the sesame oil until the fronds turn bright green.

Add the water and simmer for 30 minutes, or pressure cook for 20 minutes. (Cut these times in half if the midribs have been removed).

Ladle out some soup into a bowl. Stir in the miso. Pour and stir the miso mixture back into the pot. Turn off the heat. Taste and add more miso, if desired.

Garnish with scallions or chives, and serve.

Per serving: Calories 51, Protein 2 g, Fat 2 g, Carbohydrates 7 g,
Fiber 3 g, Calcium 52 mg, Sodium 291 mg

❖ *For a lighter soup, omit the oil and simmer the vegetables without sautéing them first. Add any thinly sliced root vegetable such as carrots, daikon, and turnip.*

❖ *When the root vegetables are tender, you can add chopped garden greens or wild greens such as watercress, collards, dandelion greens, and bok choy.*

❖ *Add cubes of tofu or seitan with freshly ground ginger or* **Nori/Ginger Sea Seasonings** *once the root vegetables are tender.*

Alaria Split Pea Soup

Yield: 4 to 6 servings

Chase the winter blues away with this hearty soup. Thanks Wendy.

1 ounce **alaria** (about ¾ cup tightly packed)
6 cups water
1½ cups split peas, rinsed
1 bay leaf
1 teaspoon cumin
1 teaspoon coriander
2 to 3 cloves garlic
1 large onion, diced
2 to 3 cups sliced carrots
1 to 2 stalks celery, chopped
2 teaspoons oregano
1 tablespoon soy sauce, or to taste

Snip the alaria into 1-inch pieces with scissors, and add to a large soup pot with the water, split peas, bay leaf, cumin, and coriander. Simmer for 50 to 60 minutes until the split peas are soft and almost ready to dissolve. Add the garlic, onion, carrots, and celery, and simmer until the vegetables are soft and brightly colored, about 20 minutes. Add the oregano and season to taste with soy sauce.

Per serving: Calories 196, Protein 12 g, Fat 1 g, Carbohydrates 37 g, Fiber 14 g, Calcium 108 mg, Sodium 473 mg

❖ *Pressure cook all the ingredients except the oregano and soy sauce for 20 minutes. Wait until the pressure comes down, and season to taste with oregano and soy sauce.*

❖ *You can sauté the vegetables before adding them to the pot.*

❖ *For a lighter soup, use only ¾ cup split peas.*

❖ *Add 4 to 8 ounces cubed tempeh when you add the vegetables.*

❖ *You can easily substitute wakame, kelp, kombu, or dulse for alaria.*

Kelp Dashi/Miso Soup

Yield: 6 servings

Dashi is commonly made with fish flakes, but here is a fabulous vegetarian version.

2½ ounces **kelp** (2½ cups)
4 to 5 dried black mushrooms
5 quarts cold water
2½ ounces sake or Xiao Xing wine
3 tablespoons tamari or soy sauce
2 tablespoons sugar
One 8-ounce package somen noodles
1 bunch greens (mizuna, mustard greens, spinach, chard)
6 tablespoons barley or rice miso
2 large scallions, sliced
8 ounces silken tofu, cut into bite-size cubes
1 sheet **toasted nori**, cut into thin strips (optional)

Soak the kelp and mushrooms in the water for 6 hours in a 6- to 8-quart stockpot. You can do this in the morning and finish the dashi later that day.

With a strainer spoon or tongs, take out the mushrooms. Discard the tough stems, cut the mushroom caps into thin julienne strips, and put them back into the pot.

Bring the kelp, mushrooms, and water to a boil. Turn the heat off and let it steep for 10 minutes. Then strain the kelp out of the stock.

Add the wine, soy sauce, and sugar. Bring the dashi back to a boil, and add the somen noodles. Stir the noodles for about 2 to 5 minutes until they are tender. Turn off the heat and add the greens. Ladle out some broth into a soup bowl, and mash in the miso, then stir the miso broth back into the pot.

Serve garnished with the tofu and scallions. Floating some strips of nori on top adds extra beauty.

Per serving: Calories 251, Protein 11 g, Fat 3 g, Carbohydrates 45 g,
Fiber 6 g, Calcium 140 mg, Sodium 2009 mg

Bouillabaisse de Legumes

Dulse and peas replace fish in this delightful soup reminiscent of the south of France. Thanks Susan. Pictured on page 65.

- 4 pounds shelling peas in pods (1 cup shelled)
- 4 tablespoons extra-virgin olive oil
- 1 cup finely chopped onions
- 6 small potatoes, boiled, peeled, and thickly sliced
- 1 sprig dried thyme (½ teaspoon)
- 1 bay leaf
- ½ teaspoon fennel seeds
- 2 to 3 grams saffron threads
- 4 tablespoons **dulse**
- 2 quarts spring water
- 1 pint plum tomatoes, crushed (with juice)
- ½ cup fruity white wine
- Sea salt to taste (optional)
- Freshly ground black pepper to taste
- Red pepper flakes to taste
- 2 tablespoons anise-flavored liqueur (optional)
- 3 cloves fresh garlic, crushed
- 12 slices toasted French or hearty country bread
- 6 organic eggs (optional)

Shell the peas and set aside.

Heat the oil in a deep, heavy saucepan. Add the onions and sauté until soft, about 5 minutes. Stir in the potatoes and the remaining ingredients except the peas, liqueur, garlic, bread, and eggs. Simmer over low heat, partially covered, for 10 minutes.

Add the peas and cook until the potatoes are just done, about 10 minutes. Do not overcook! Stir in the anise-flavored liqueur, if using. Taste and adjust the salt and pepper.

Rub the toasted bread with the crushed garlic if desired. Break the eggs directly into the soup, and poach gently a few minutes.

To serve, place 2 slices of toast in a heated shallow soup bowl. Ladle in the soup and top with a poached egg.

Per serving: Calories 297, Protein 7 g, Fat 10 g, Carbohydrates 42 g, Fiber 5 g, Calcium 69 mg, Sodium 348 mg

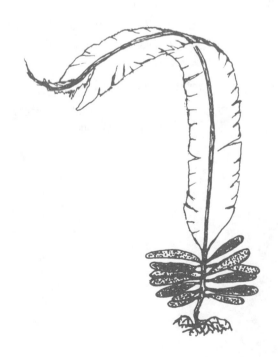

Dulse Chowder

Yield: 4 servings

Here is simple and sustaining chowder from Linnette's kitchen. The trick here is to add the dulse just a few minutes before the end of cooking. The dulse will separate, yet retain its color and texture.

1 cup water
1 medium onion, diced
2 to 3 medium potatoes, chopped
1 ounce (about ½ package) **dulse**
½ pound fresh or frozen corn
1 quart plain soymilk (not lite)
White or yellow miso to taste
Black pepper to taste
¼ to ½ teaspoon tarragon (optional)

In a medium pot, bring 1 cup water to a boil.

Add the onion and potatoes, and cook for 5 to 10 minutes. Add the dulse and corn, and cook for 1 minute.

Add the soymilk and reduce the heat to a simmer. (Do not boil the soymilk or it will curdle.) Stir occasionally. The dulse will separate into pieces after a few minutes.

Add the miso, pepper, and tarragon, stir, and serve.

Per serving: Calories 233, Protein 12 g, Fat 5 g, Carbohydrates 40 g, Fiber 9 g, Calcium 38 mg, Sodium 160 mg

SALADS

Making Sea Vegetable Salads

Gourmets and natural food enthusiasts recognize that mineral-rich sea vegetables add an exotic touch to salads. They are a beautiful contrast to brightly colored vegetables like carrots, red cabbage, and beets. Soft like noodles, marinated sea vegetable salads are fun to eat and very tasty. Mixing and matching wild sea vegetables with land vegetables helps you go beyond the conventional pasta and bean salad.

Select from a number of sea vegetables such as dulse, sea palm, arame, alaria, wakame, hiziki, and kelp. You might make your choice based on how soon you want to eat. Dulse and smoked dulse are like sun-dried tomatoes; you can add them directly to a salad or marinate first. Mild-flavored arame needs a 5-minute presoak and then it is ready for salad. Other thicker and stronger ocean-flavored sea vegetables like hiziki benefit from both pre-soaking as well as cooking to soften and mellow out their flavor before dressing them up with flavorful vinaigrettes or creamy dressings. You can also deep fry wakame (as well as other sea vegetables) crumble, and add to salads. If you are in a hurry, try sea vegetable sprinkles or flakes. They make great garnishes for salads too.

Around the world, salads come alive with sea vegetables—fruity Mediterranean, sweet and sour Asian, picnic-friendly American.

How to Use Sea Vegetables in Salads

Alaria: Hearty alaria needs to become tender. There are lots of ways to prepare it for salad. To soften without cooking, soak or marinate the fronds at least 12 hours. (Watch them grow 50% in size!)

To tenderize and turn bright green, blanch the fronds briefly, steam for 10 minutes, or pressure cook for 5 minutes. Chop into bite-size pieces and toss with salad greens.

Arame: First look over the arame and remove any tiny seashells, rare as it is to find one. Give it a quick rinse to remove any sand.

Then soak arame in enough water to cover for 5 minutes. For example, soak ½ cup of arame in 1 cup of water. Discard the soaking water or save for soup stock, dressings, or dilute with water and use as a fertilizer to feed plants. Place arame in a mixing bowl, and add other salad ingredients. Dress with toasted sesame or regular sesame oil, rice vinegar, umeboshi vinegar, or tamari for a delicious Asian-style salad. Since arame is black, thin, and noodle-like, it looks wonderful with brightly colored vegetables such as red cabbage, red radishes, scallions, beets, and carrots. Smoked, raw, or fried tofu also adds to the fun.

Quick Asian Salad—Presoak arame in water for 5 minutes. Discard the excess water or use for dressing. Slice red and green cabbage, a bunch of scallions, or red onion. Add sliced carrots and radishes. Dress with toasted sesame oil, rice vinegar, tamari or umeboshi vinegar. You can create quick and easy variations with garden greens, cooked noodles, and cubed tofu.

Dulse: Dulse lets you be spontaneous. Add dulse leaves to salads like spinach or lettuce. You can also marinate dulse with dressings before adding it to a salad. Pan-fry it first for a bacon-like flavor and aroma. Dulse is a natural in Caesar, Greek, Waldorf, potato, and garden salads. Try smoked dulse for a delicious smoky sea taste.

Hiziki: Like arame, hiziki needs a quick rinse to remove foreign matter like sand or shells. Hiziki has a spaghetti-like texture and is thicker than arame. Presoak hiziki for 10 minutes before adding to salad. Hiziki has a stronger ocean flavor than most sea vegetables. Most cooks prefer to sauté or boil hiziki for 35 minutes after presoaking to mellow its flavor. Hiziki salads look great with bright greens like watercress or steamed broccoli. Creamy tofu dressings over hiziki are cool and attractive on a hot summer day.

Kelp: Uncooked kelp is chewy until soaked or marinated. To fully tenderize kelp, simmer for 15 to 20 minutes, pressure cook 5 minutes, roast for 3 to 4 minutes at 300°F, or pan fry for 4 to 5 minutes until crisp. You could also soak kelp for an hour or marinate for 1 to 24 hours. Keep in mind that kelp expands 40% in liquid and will absorb up to five times its weight. A little goes a long way. Add tender kelp to salads or better yet, cook beans with kelp and then add it along with your cooked beans to any bean salad. You can also make kelp pickles (page 49).

Laver: First check for tiny pebbles or shells, and discard them. Lightly roast for 5 to 8 minutes in a 300ºF oven until crisp, or dry roast in a dry skillet, turning occasionally until crisp before adding to salad. To tenderize without roasting or cooking, marinate laver for at least 18 hours.

Once cooked or marinated, add chopped laver to pasta and bean salads, green salads, or your favorite dressing. You can also crumble roasted laver over your salad for a strong flavored garnish.

Sea Palm: The fettuccini of sea vegetables is wonderful in salads with and without noodles. Add it fresh or presoak dried sea palm for 5 minutes in about thee to four times the amount of water; then watch it triple in size. Sauté in oil (sesame oil, for example) or simmer it covered in water or stock for 10 to 45 minutes. The longer the time, the softer and more noodle-like it gets. Combine it with multicolored peppers for a beautiful salad. Season it with fresh citrus juice such as lime, lemon, or orange.

Beautiful Salad—Presoak and cook sea palm (as described above) in water to cover till tender. Add fresh snow peas and sliced red peppers. Dress with fresh lime juice, sesame oil, cilantro, and tamari.

Wakame: Fresh wakame is wonderful in a salad. If you have dry wakame, it is best to presoak it for 10 minutes or until tender. Then boil it for 15 minutes before adding it to a salad. Cucumbers and radishes are classic in wakame salad. Try dressing wakame salads with garlic, ginger, honey, sesame oil, and tamari for a sweet Asian-style salad.

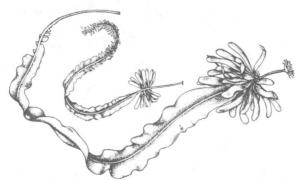

Sea Palm Salad

Yield: 4 servings

A beautiful and delicious salad that really showcases the delicate flavor of sea palm, nicely complemented by a light, vinaigrette-type dressing. Thanks Christina.

1 cup **sea palm**, soaked and sliced into bite-size pieces
Spring or filtered water
Soy sauce
1 cup corn kernels
1 carrot, diced
½ red onion, diced
½ red bell pepper, roasted and diced

Italian Dressing
1 clove garlic, peeled
¼ cup extra-virgin olive oil
Dash of soy sauce
1 onion, grated
2 umeboshi plums, pitted
2 to 3 tablespoons balsamic vinegar
Dried basil or rosemary to taste

Dice the soaked sea palm, and place it in a small saucepan with enough water to cover halfway. Sprinkle with soy sauce and bring to a boil. Reduce the heat, cover, and simmer until tender, about 35 minutes. Remove the lid and allow any remaining liquid to cook away.

Cook the corn, carrot, and onion separately in the order listed. Add each vegetable to boiling water, bring back to a boil, remove the vegetable with a slotted spoon, then cool it in iced water. Drain the vegetables well, and mix in a bowl with the bell pepper.

To make the dressing, rub the garlic on the bottom of a suribachi (grinding bowl). Warm the olive oil and a dash of soy sauce in a small saucepan over low heat for 3 to 4 minutes. Combine the oil mixture and the remaining dressing ingredients in a grinding bowl, and grind until smooth. (If a grinding bowl isn't available, use a mortar and pestle, or combine in a blender.)

Toss the cooked sea palm and cooked vegetables with the Italian dressing, and marinate 30 minutes, allowing the flavors to fully develop. Serve at room temperature or slightly warm.

Per serving: Calories 200, Protein 3 g, Fat 14 g, Carbohydrates 19 g, Fiber 5 g, Calcium 77 mg, Sodium 235 mg

Marinated Wakame & Vegetables

Yield: 4 to 6 servings

A quick and easy vegetable dish with a zesty marinated taste. Thanks Christina.

Spring or filtered water
½ cup matchstick-size carrot pieces
1 head cauliflower, cut into small florets
4 or 5 snow peas, trimmed and left whole
½ cup **wakame**, soaked 3 minutes and diced

Marinade
Juice of 1 lime
¼ cup brown rice vinegar
1 teaspoon soy sauce
1 tablespoon balsamic vinegar
Spring or filtered water

Bring a pot of water to a boil. Separately cook each vegetable until crisp-tender, carrots for about 30 seconds, cauliflower for about 4 minutes, and snow peas for about 30 seconds. Drain well and mix with the wakame.

Mix together the marinade ingredients, adding only enough water to gentle the flavor of the marinade but not enough to make it watery. Toss the vegetables with the marinade, and let them marinate for about 30 minutes to allow the flavors to develop. Toss gently just before serving.

Per serving: Calories 42, Protein 3 g, Fat 0 g, Carbohydrates 9 g, Fiber 4 g, Calcium 53 mg, Sodium 186 mg

Hiziki Ribbon Salad

Yield: 4 servings

This is a strong-tasting salad, nicely balanced with tender vegetables and a light citrus dressing. I serve this in small amounts as a complementary dish to round out a meal. Thanks Christina.

- 1 cup **hiziki**, rinsed well and soaked until tender (about 10 minutes)
- Spring or filtered water
- Dash of soy sauce
- 1 tablespoon mirin
- 3 or 4 red radishes, thinly sliced
- Umeboshi vinegar
- 1 cup French cut green beans
- 1 yellow summer squash, cut into matchsticks
- Juice of 1 lemon

Place the hiziki in a small saucepan with just enough water to cover. Add a dash of soy sauce and a dash of the mirin. Simmer, uncovered for about 25 minutes until tender. If the water evaporates too quickly, add a bit more and reduce the heat so the hiziki can cook thoroughly. Cooking hiziki uncovered gentles its strong flavor and brings out its natural sweetness.

While the hiziki is cooking, place the radish slices in a small bowl, and cover with umeboshi vinegar. Allow it to marinate for 15 minutes. Bring a small pan of water to a boil, and separately boil the green beans and squash until just tender (about 10 minutes for the green beans and 3 to 4 minutes for the squash). Cool in iced water, drain, and set aside.

When the hiziki is tender and the cooking liquid has completely evaporated, remove it from the heat. Add the mirin, toss gently, and allow it to cool to room temperature before stirring in the marinated radishes, blanched vegetables, and lemon juice. Serve chilled or at room temperature.

Per serving: Calories 40, Protein 2 g, Fat 0 g, Carbohydrates 8 g, Fiber 3 g, Calcium 78 mg, Sodium 207 mg

Dulse Chick-Pea Salad

Yield: 4 to 6 servings

Here is a personal favorite of the Maine Coast Sea Vegetables Company. It is a recipe we choose when we want to show off our mineral-rich dulse. Pictured on the cover.

1 large whole wheat pita bread, or corn or other whole grain tortilla, ripped into small pieces
1½ cups cooked chick-peas
1 cup chopped **dulse**
1 cucumber, peeled and diced
1 tomato, diced
½ cup chopped black olives
¼ cup lemon juice
½ cup chopped parsley or cilantro
2 cloves garlic, grated
⅛ to ¼ cup olive oil
½ cup sliced or diced Vidalia onions
1 cup chopped romaine or leaf lettuce

Preheat the oven or toaster oven to 400°F. Bake the pita bread for 5 minutes. Put in a large mixing bowl with the rest of the ingredients, stir well, and serve.

Per serving: Calories 242, Protein 8 g, Fat 12 g, Carbohydrates 27 g, Fiber 7 g, Calcium 89 mg, Sodium 250 mg

Carrot & Parsnip Salad with Smoked Dulse

Yield: 10 servings (5 cups)

Smoked dulse gives this salad a wonderful smoky flavor, and if all you have on hand is regular dulse, go ahead and make this salad anyway. It is quick and easy to prepare. Thanks to award-winning chef Ken Bergeron.

- 2 cups grated carrots
- 2 cups grated parsnips
- ¾ cup finely diced celery (1 or 2 stalks)
- 1 tablespoon minced red onion
- 2 tablespoons **smoked dulse**, toasted and crumbled
- 2 teaspoons apple cider vinegar
- 2 teaspoons prepared mustard
- 1 tablespoon chopped parsley
- 2 tablespoons sunflower seeds

Combine all the ingredients, mix well, and season to taste.

Per serving: Calories 49, Protein 1 g, Fat 1 g, Carbohydrates 9 g, Fiber 2 g, Calcium 23 mg, Sodium 33 mg

New Potato Salad

Yield: 4 to 6 servings

Here is an all-American-style potato salad you can have fun with by changing the dressing each time you make it. For instance, curry powder adds an Indian accent, and you can add extra cayenne and ginger to make it very spicy for those that like it hot.

8 cups cubed potatoes (3 pounds)
½ cup firmly packed **dulse**
1 large onion or 2 medium red onions, sliced
1 to 2 tablespoons olive oil or soy mayonnaise
2 to 3 tablespoons lemon juice
1 tablespoon dry dill weed, or 2 to 3 fresh sprigs, chopped
1½ cups chopped celery (about 3 to 4 stalks)
1 tablespoon mustard powder
½ cup bread and butter pickles
1 tablespoon juice from pickles
1 hard-boiled egg, sliced (optional)
Pesto for garnish (optional)
Chopped fresh cilantro for garnish (optional)

Simmer the potatoes for 15 to 20 minutes in enough water to cover. Do not overcook. Rinse with cold water to cool.

Pull apart the dulse and either bake at 350ºF for 3 to 5 minutes, or pan fry dry, stirring. The dulse will crisp up and turn color when done. (Do not burn.)

Place the onion, olive oil, lemon juice, dill, and celery in a large mixing bowl, cover, and let marinate while the potatoes cook.

Add the potatoes to the marinated vegetables. Add the mustard powder, pickles, pickle juice, and hard-boiled egg, and mix lightly. Crumble the roasted dulse over the salad, and mix in.

Per serving: Calories 329, Protein 7 g, Fat 5 g, Carbohydrates 67 g, Fiber 7 g, Calcium 40 mg, Sodium 287 mg

❖ *Add 1½ to 2 tablespoons curry powder for an Indian accent.*

❖ *If you like it spicy, add 2 teaspoons grated ginger or 1 teaspoon ginger powder, as well as 1 teaspoon cumin, ¼ teaspoon turmeric, and ¼ teaspoon cayenne. Adjust the seasonings to suit your taste.*

❖ *You can also change the dressing to garlic mayonnaise, tofu mayonnaise, or other flavors of store bought or homemade mayonnaise.*

Marinated Sea Palm with Roasted Red Peppers

Yield: 3 to 4 servings

Stephen Yundt, Chef of the Bluebird Café in Hopland, California, gave us this one. He says that it is a "perfect garnish for seafood dishes and rice . . . colorful, flavorful, nutritionally wholesome, and a conversation piece!" This may be made two days in advance, if you like.

1 cup tightly packed **sea palm fronds** (1 ounce)
1 quart boiling water
2 red bell peppers, roasted, peeled, and sliced
½ cup sesame oil or toasted sesame oil
2 teaspoons black pepper
3 tablespoons honey
4 tablespoons balsamic vinegar
4 cloves garlic, minced
2 tablespoons minced fresh gingerroot
2 tablespoons chopped fresh cilantro

Boil the sea palm fronds in water for 2 to 3 minutes until tenderized yet still slightly crunchy, like a land vegetable. Drain and plunge in cold water to stop the cooking. Drain again and if you like, save the cooking water for another use such as soup stock, cooking beans or grains, and even to water plants, once it cools.

In a large salad bowl, add the sea palm fronds and all the remaining ingredients, and toss. Let marinate for at least 4 hours before serving.

Per serving: Calories 325, Protein 2 g, Fat 2 g, Carbohydrates 12 g, Fiber 3 g, Calcium 95 mg, Sodium 313 mg

Sushi Salad

Yield: 8 servings

Very sensual in the making, it's delicious, simple, and beautiful. Serving sushi salad on a bed of lettuce, garnished with slices of red and green bell peppers, makes this a work of art. Eleanor, the creator of this recipe, says, "It has been prepared this way for a senior center fundraiser by Chef Stephen Yundt, using wild rice, and even the cowboys loved it!"

½ to 1 cup flaked roasted **nori** (see roasting instructions below)
2 teaspoons roasted sesame oil
8 cups cooked rice, cooled
1 teaspoon grated or crushed ginger
3 tablespoons diced onions or green onions
1 tablespoon sesame seeds (optional)
1 tablespoon honey
1 teaspoon rice wine or vinegar
4 tablespoons soy sauce, or to taste
4 to 6 cloves garlic, crushed
Parsley and/or cilantro
Lettuce
Diced red and green bell peppers, and/or grated zucchini

To roast the nori, pull the sheets apart and fry in a pan over medium heat for 4 to 5 minutes until crisp, pressing occasionally with a spatula or spoon until crumbly. Or set in a 300ºF toaster oven for 5 to 8 minutes.

Combine all the ingredients, except the lettuce and bell peppers, adding the roasted nori and parsley last. Reserve ⅛ cup nori and ¼ cup parsley and/or cilantro for garnish. Adjust the ingredients to taste. Serve on a bed of lettuce garnished with the peppers and/or grated zucchini and nori flakes.

Per serving: Calories 242, Protein 6 g, Fat 2 g, Carbohydrates 50 g, Fiber 2 g, Calcium 30 mg, Sodium 508 mg

Orange Wakame Salad

Yield: 4 servings

This delicious salad is ready in 10 minutes. Thanks Eden Foods.

> 3 tablespoons Eden Wakame Flakes, soaked in 2 cups of hot water
> ¼ cup Eden Mirin
> ½ teaspoon sea salt
> 1 cucumber, thinly sliced
> 2 oranges or tangerines, peeled and sliced
> 5 red radishes, cut in half and sliced
> 1 green onion, sliced
> 2 tablespoons black sesame seeds or Eden Shake (Furikake)
> 2 tablespoons Eden Brown Rice Vinegar

Soak the wakame in water for 10 minutes. Drain and add mirin and sea salt. Mix in the cucumber, oranges, radishes, green onion, sesame seeds, and brown rice vinegar. Serve chilled.

Per serving: Calories 81, Protein 2 g, Fat 2 g, Carbohydrates 12 g, Fiber 3 g, Calcium 95 mg, Sodium 313 mg

❖ *If wakame flakes are not available, you can substitute whole wakame or alaria, well cooked and finely chopped. See page 81 for cooking instructions.*

Alaria-Green Bean Salad

Yield: 4 servings

Two 4- to 5-inch strips **alaria**
2 cups water
4 cups fresh green beans
2 to 3 cups mung bean sprouts
2 carrots, grated
2 to 4 cloves garlic, minced

Dressing
2 to 3 tablespoons rice syrup
2 tablespoons soy sauce
½ teaspoon sesame oil
½ cup reserved broth (from cooking alaria)

Simmer the alaria in the water for 30 minutes, or pressure cook for 15 minutes. Reserve the broth for making the dressing. Cut the alaria into small pieces, omitting the hard center midrib, if desired. Put it in a frying pan with the green beans, mung bean sprouts, carrots, and garlic.

In a small pan, combine the dressing ingredients. Heat briefly, then pour over the vegetables. Cover and steam for 5 to 6 minutes. Serve hot with rice or chill and serve as a salad.

Per serving: Calories 127, Protein 6 g, Fat 1 g, Carbohydrates 28 g,
Fiber 7 g, Calcium 91 mg, Sodium 639 mg

Cucumber Sea Vegetable Salad

Yield: 4 to 6 servings

Asian seasonings and four different sea veggies make this the king of sea-veggie salads.

¼ ounce **alaria** (about ¼ cup)
½ ounce **kelp** (about ½ cup)
1 cup water
½ ounce **dulse** (about ½ cup)
¼ ounce **laver** (about ½ cup)
3 tablespoons brown rice vinegar
3 tablespoons mirin
1 tablespoon toasted sesame oil
1 tablespoon tamari
2 teaspoons freshly grated ginger
1½ teaspoons toasted sesame seeds
2 to 3 medium cucumbers, peeled and cut into
    long or short bite-size strips
Chopped scallions, parsley, or slices of sweet red pepper for
    garnish (optional)

Pressure cook the alaria and kelp for 10 minutes in 1 cup water, or simmer gently in 2 cups water for 20 minutes. While they are cooking, scissor-snip the dulse into small pieces. Pull apart the laver and toast it lightly in a skillet over medium heat while stirring and crushing until crisp and fragrant.

In a large mixing bowl, whisk together the vinegar, mirin, sesame oil, tamari, ginger, and sesame seeds. Mix in the cucumbers and set aside.

Cut the kelp into small squares or diamonds. Strip the alaria leaf from its midrib, and chop small. Add the dulse and laver, and mix with the cucumbers. Chill and marinate a few hours. Taste, adjust the seasonings, garnish, and serve.

Per serving: Calories 72, Protein 4 g, Fat 3 g, Carbohydrates 9 g,
Fiber 42 g, Calcium 80 mg, Sodium 443 mg

❖ *Drizzle on hot pepper oil for a spicy dish.*

Mediterranean Salad with Dulse

Yield: 4 servings

This fruity salad made by Sharon Rhoads highlights dulse and kelp. Pictured on page 66.

Dressing
⅓ cup safflower oil
2 tablespoons olive oil
2 tablespoons vinegar
1 to 2 tablespoons lemon juice
½ teaspoon oregano
½ teaspoon cumin powder
½ teaspoon **Kelp Granules** or **Kelp/Cayenne Sea Seasonings**
Freshly ground black pepper to taste

Salad
3 to 4 citrus fruits, peeled and chunked
1 cup **dulse**, rinsed and drained
Bed of salad greens
Rings of raw purple onion for garnish

Toss the fruits with the dulse and dressing. Marinate for 15 minutes. Arrange on salad greens and top with the onion.

Per serving: Calories 296, Protein 3 g, Fat 24 g, Carbohydrates 19 g,
Fiber 5 g, Calcium 79 mg, Sodium 97 mg

Waldorf Salad with Dulse

Yield: 6 servings

Choose one of the two different dressings, and score big with crowd-pleasing Waldorf Salad.

Salad
1 head red leaf lettuce, chopped or broken into pieces
1 cup chopped **dulse**
2 apples cut into chunks (2 cups)
3 grated carrots
1 cup chopped celery
½ cup chopped roasted pecans, or ½ cup walnuts
¼ cup raisins (optional)

Asian-Style Dressing
¼ cup soy mayonnaise
2 tablespoons brown rice vinegar
1 teaspoon umeboshi paste

Western-Style Dressing
⅔ cup salad oil
Juice of 1 lemon
4 tablespoons soy sauce

Combine all the salad ingredients. Whisk together the dressing ingredients, and mix gently into the salad. Allow the salad to marinate for 20 minutes before serving to allow the dulse to absorb moisture and soften.

Note: If the salad must be served immediately, lightly rinse the dulse after cutting it.

Per serving (Asian-Style): Calories 146, Protein 3 g, Fat 9 g, Carbohydrates 16 g, Fiber 5 g, Calcium 41 mg, Sodium 199 mg

Per serving (Western-Style): Calories 335, Protein 4 g, Fat 30 g, Carbohydrates 16 g, Fiber 5 g, Calcium 37 mg, Sodium 715 mg

Notuna Salad

Yield: 4 to 6 servings

Tuna salad can be salty and high in fat. Commercial tuna, mayo, and pickles are all loaded with added salt. Our vegan version has only natural sodium from mineral-rich dulse and kelp and no added oil. It is a "Dolphin's Delight."

Two 12.3-ounce boxes extra-firm silken tofu
⅝ cup firmly packed **kelp**, cut into bite-size pieces
⅝ cup firmly packed **dulse**, cut into bite-size pieces
⅝ cup finely chopped celery
⅝ cup chopped sweet onion
2½ to 3½ tablespoons umeboshi vinegar,
    rice wine, or cider vinegar
1¼ teaspoons mirin (optional)
2½ to 3½ teaspoons **Dulse/Garlic Sea Seasonings**
Freshly ground white pepper to taste

Freeze the unopened boxes of tofu for at least 12 hours. Remove from the freezer and let them defrost almost completely, leaving some ice crystals on the tofu. Press gently, pour off any accumulated water, and flake into pieces. Toss with the kelp, dulse, and chopped vegetables. Combine the vinegar, mirin, dulse granules, and pepper, and drizzle it on the salad. Taste and adjust the seasonings, if desired.

Note: If time permits, prepare this 1 or 2 days in advance to let the flavors meld. Cover tightly and refrigerate; it keeps at least one week. Drain off the excess liquid before serving.

Per serving: Calories 111, Protein 11 g, Fat 4 g, Carbohydrates 9 g,
Fiber 4 g, Calcium 83 mg, Sodium 243 mg

❖ *If you are avoiding soy, you can substitute seitan for tofu, and proceed as above without freezing.*

❖ *Add 2 tablespoons pickled capers or chopped sweet or sour pickles.*

❖ *Add seeds from one papaya, and save the fruit for dessert.*

❖ *Add 2 tablespoons mild olive oil or sesame oil.*

Beet Horseradish Salad

Yield: 4 servir

Carl Karush of Maine Coast Sea Vegetables says, "Yes, this recipe serves ⌡
as a small side dish and probably more just as a condiment (on 2 or 3 slice⌐ ⌐⌡
bread, crackers, etc.). For a salad portion I'd say double it. Dulse and sprouts
make a quick and easy salad." This was developed by his wife Wendy.

3 medium beets, scrubbed clean with a vegetable brush
  (about 2 cups)
3 tablespoons sour cream or yogurt
2 to 3 tablespoons prepared horseradish, or
  4 to 6 tablespoons freshly grated horseradish
¼ cup chopped **dulse**
¼ teaspoon honey
Pepper, to taste

Cook the unpeeled beets in boiling water for 15 to 20 minutes. Peel the beets by holding them under cold water and rubbing the skins off. Slice the beets into strips or small cubes.

Combine the remaining ingredients in a large mixing bowl. Add the beets, mix, and chill.

Per serving: Calories 177, Protein 5 g, Fat 8 g, Carbohydrates 24 g,
Fiber 5 g, Calcium 100 mg, Sodium 265 mg

Dulse Sprout Salad

Yield: 4 servings

1 cup **dulse**, rinsed and cut into bite-size pieces
4 cups your favorite sprouts
½ cup sliced scallions
½ cup red peppers
1 stalk celery, sliced
½ cup chopped avocado
2 teaspoons lemon juice
2 teaspoons tamari

Combine all the ingredients together. Taste and adjust the seasonings, if desired.

Per serving: Calories 74, Protein 4 g, Fat 4 g, Carbohydrates 8 g,
Fiber 5 g, Calcium 39 mg, Sodium 274 mg

Salsa Sea Salad

Yield: 4 servings

Here's a sensuous salad you can either make mostly from scratch or simply add alaria to your favorite salsa.

½ cup **alaria**
1 to 2 teaspoons vegetable oil
1 ripe avocado, peeled, seeded, and cut into small dice
1 ripe tomato, diced (remove seeds)
Juice of 1 lime, or 1 tablespoon lemon juice
3 scallions, minced
3 tablespoons cilantro or parsley, minced
3 tablespoons low-sodium salsa
Dash of hot sauce (optional)

Check the alaria for small shells, then scissor-snip the alaria into ½-inch strips across the width.

Place the alaria pieces on a lightly oiled baking tray. Roast in a 300°F oven for 3 to 5 minutes, stirring once or twice. The alaria is done when it slightly changes color and becomes crisp. Remove from the tray and set aside.

In a mixing bowl, combine the avocado, tomato, lime juice, scallions, cilantro, salsa, and hot sauce. Toss gently.

When serving, crumble the roasted alaria over the salad, and mix gently.

Serve on mixed salad greens, use as stuffing in pita bread, add to tacos or tortillas, or serve with chips or beans and rice.

Per serving: Calories 122, Protein 2 g, Fat 9 g, Carbohydrates 11 g,
Fiber 4 g, Calcium 49 mg, Sodium 123 mg

Kelp/Cayenne Vinaigrette

3 parts olive oil
1 part vinegar
½ part **Kelp/Cayenne Sea Seasonings**

Whip together all the ingredients. Add a dash of fresh or dried rosemary or thyme, if you wish.

Sesame Laver Salad Dressing

Yield: 4 to 6 servings

For those of you trying to introduce sea vegetables into your family's diet, here's a delicious dressing to get you off to a good start.

1 cup **laver,** or 3 tablespoons **Nori Granules Sea Seasonings**
3 tablespoons roasted sesame seeds
4 tablespoons brown rice vinegar
1 cup water
½ teaspoon soy sauce

Preheat the oven to 300°F. Toast the laver for 5 to 8 minutes until crisp, or dry roast it in a medium skillet, turning occasionally, until crisp. Crumble the roasted laver and grind it together coarsely with the roasted sesame seeds in a mill, suribachi, or blender. Transfer to a bottle or jar with the rest of the ingredients. Shake vigorously. Serve as a dressing on grain, noodle, or vegetable salads.

Per serving: Calories 35, Protein 1 g, Fat 3 g, Carbohydrates 2 g, Fiber 1 g, Calcium 57 mg, Sodium 36 mg

Wild Tahini Dressing

Yield: 4 to 6 servings

Dulse's iron-rich taste compliments any lettuce-based salad. Here's a simple dressing from Montse Bradford.

- ½ cup water
- 2 tablespoons tahini
- 1 tablespoon umeboshi plum paste
- ½ cup finely sliced **dulse**, soaked in water for 10 minutes and drained
- 3 scallions, finely chopped

Warm the water, add the tahini, and stir until creamy. Stir or blend in the umeboshi paste thoroughly. Stir in the dulse and scallions and/or parsley or watercress.

Per serving: Calories 49, Protein 2 g, Fat 3 g, Carbohydrates 4 g, Fiber 2 g, Calcium 38 mg, Sodium 169 mg

VEGETABLE DISHES

Sesame Carrots

Yield: 4 servings

A colorful, sensuous sauté from Linnette.

Two 5-inch strips **kelp**
¾ cup water
4 medium carrots
1 tablespoon toasted sesame oil
½ teaspoon mirin (optional)
1 teaspoon roasted sesame seeds for garnish

Soak the kelp in the water for 5 to 10 minutes until soft. Then simmer for 20 minutes or pressure cook for 10 minutes in the same water. Set aside.

Slice the carrots on the diagonal to about ½ inch thick or less. Slice the kelp into thin strips.

Heat a heavy skillet. Add the oil, carrots, and mirin. Sauté for about 5 minutes.

Add the sliced kelp and kelp cooking water to the carrots. Cover and simmer for 5 to 10 minutes, stirring occasionally, until both the carrots and the kelp are tender. Taste and adjust the seasonings. Garnish with roasted sesame seeds.

Per serving: Calories 72, Protein 1 g, Fat 4 g, Carbohydrates 9 g, Fiber 3 g, Calcium 52 mg, Sodium 144 mg

❖ *Substitute sea palm, kombu, arame, or hiziki for the kelp. For example, you can use ½ cup dried sea palm, firmly packed. Soak it for 5 to 10 minutes, and cut it into 1-inch long pieces. Add the sea palm to the carrots with soaking water as needed.*

❖ *For another delicious variation, add some fresh or dried shiitakes, or try a colorful combination of five seasonal vegetables such as onions, carrots, delicata squash, celery, burdock, turnip, or cabbage.*

❖ *Add some spices like garlic and ginger. For a spicier version, add chile pepper and garnish with chopped cilantro to balance the heat.*

Fresh Daikon & Kombu in Orange Sauce

Yield: 4 servings

A refreshingly clean-tasting dish. Thanks Christina.

Spring or filtered water
One 6-inch piece **kombu**, soaked for about 5 minutes or
    until tender and cut into thin pieces
1 medium daikon, cut into ½-inch rounds

Orange Sauce
Juice and grated zest of 1 orange
1 teaspoon umeboshi vinegar
1 teaspoon balsamic vinegar

Bring about 1 inch of water to a boil in a small saucepan. Add the kombu and cook over low heat for about 10 minutes. Remove the kombu with a strainer, and cook the daikon rounds in the same water until just tender, about 10 minutes. Drain and combine the daikon with the kombu. Arrange on a serving platter, and make the sauce.

Whisk together all the sauce ingredients in a small bowl, and spoon over the hot daikon and kombu. Marinate for 15 to 20 minutes. Chill before serving.

Per serving: Calories 35, Protein 1 g, Fat 0 g, Carbohydrates 8 g,
Fiber 3 g, Calcium 53 mg, Sodium 96 mg

Arame Sauté

Yield: 2 or 3 servings

A quick and delicious dish chock-full of lightly cooked vegetables, accented with arame. Thanks Christina.

½ cup **arame**
Spring or filtered water
Soy sauce
1 teaspoon mirin
1 teaspoon dark sesame oil
2 or 3 shallots, diced
2 cups button mushrooms, brushed clean and thinly sliced
1 cup matchstick-size carrot pieces
2 or 3 stalks broccoli, florets and stems diced
2 tablespoons sunflower seeds, lightly pan-toasted

Rinse the arame well and set aside. It will soften in a few minutes without soaking.

Place the arame in a small saucepan with enough water to cover halfway. Bring to a boil, cover, and cook over low heat for 15 minutes. Season lightly with soy sauce and mirin, and cook until all the liquid has been absorbed.

Heat the oil in a skillet over medium heat. Add the shallots and cook, stirring until translucent, about 5 minutes. Add the mushrooms and cook, stirring, until wilted. Add the carrots and cook, stirring, for 1 to 2 minutes. Finally, stir in the broccoli, and season lightly with more soy sauce. Cover and cook over low heat until the broccoli is bright green and crisp-tender, about 4 minutes. Stir in the arame and sunflower seeds. Transfer to a bowl and serve warm.

Per serving: Calories 184, Protein 9 g, Fat 8 g, Carbohydrates 24 g,
Fiber 8 g, Calcium 160 mg, Sodium 134 mg

Vinegared Hiziki

Yield: 4 servings

A small amount of this zesty strong dish will go a long way. Thanks Christina.

½ cup **hiziki**, soaked for 10 minutes
Spring or filtered water
Soy sauce
½ red bell pepper, roasted over an open flame, peeled, seeded, and diced
1 cup diced watercress
2 tablespoons brown rice vinegar
Juice of 1 lemon

Place the soaked hiziki in a saucepan with enough water to cover halfway. Season lightly with soy sauce, and bring to a boil. Reduce the heat and simmer, uncovered, for 5 minutes. Cover and cook 30 minutes more. Add the bell pepper, cover, and simmer for 5 more minutes. Remove the cover and cook away any remaining liquid. Remove the pan from the heat. Toss the watercress into the hot hiziki, then stir in the vinegar and lemon juice. Transfer to a bowl and serve warm.

Per serving: Calories 16, Protein 1 g, Fat 0 g, Carbohydrates 4 g,
Fiber 1 g, Calcium 42 mg, Sodium 105 mg

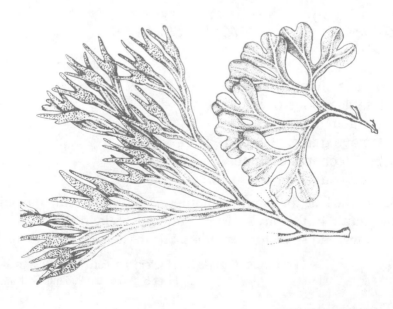

Dulse & Kale Casserole

Yield: 4 servings

Here are two versions of this super-high-calcium dish, this one with Swiss cheese and the one below with cashews.

- 8 cups chopped kale, rinsed
- 1 onion, chopped
- 1 clove garlic, chopped
- 2 tablespoons butter or olive oil
- 1 cup milk or cream
- ½ teaspoon cumin
- ½ teaspoon 5-spice powder
- ½ cup chopped **dulse**
- ½ to ¾ cup grated Swiss cheese
- 1½ cups crumbled fresh bread

Preheat the oven to 350ºF. Steam the kale for about 10 minutes. Sauté the onion and garlic in the butter for 5 minutes until translucent. Add the kale and the remaining ingredients to the onion and garlic. Stir together. Cover and bake for 15 to 20 minutes.

Per serving: Calories 283, Protein 16 g, Fat 12 g, Carbohydrates 32 g, Fiber 5 g, Calcium 492 mg, Sodium 336 mg

Dairy-Free Quick Kale

Yield: 4 servings

- 8 cups chopped kale
- 2 tablespoons olive oil
- 1 onion, chopped
- 1 clove garlic, chopped
- ½ cup chopped **dulse**
- ½ cup cashews

Steam the kale for about 10 minutes. Drain well. Sauté the onion and garlic in the olive oil for 5 minutes. Stir in the dulse and cashews, and sauté for 4 minutes. Stir in the kale and serve.

Per serving: Calories 258, Protein 9 g, Fat 17 g, Carbohydrates 24 g, Fiber 5 g, Calcium 206 mg, Sodium 109 mg

Kelp Hot Potatoes

Yield: 4 servings

Potato lovers will go for this one.

3 tablespoons soy sauce
1 tablespoon honey
6 potatoes (white or sweet)
2½ to 3 tablespoons olive oil
1 cup tightly packed **kelp** (about 1 ounce), lightly rinsed
1 cup water

Combine the soy sauce and honey in a small bowl. Mix well and set aside.

Cut the potatoes into bite-size pieces, and sauté in the oil until golden, stirring often.

Cut the kelp into pieces approximately 1 inch long, and add to potatoes. Add the soy-honey mixture and stir thoroughly. Add the water, cover, and simmer for 15 to 20 minutes.

Per serving: Calories 296, Protein 6 g, Fat 10 g, Carbohydrates 48 g, Fiber 6 g, Calcium 63 mg, Sodium 999 mg

Stir-Fried Cauliflower

Yield: 8 servings

This Asian-style stir-fry is best served over steamed rice or noodles. Thanks Susan.

- 1½ tablespoons peanut oil
- 2 tablespoons finely chopped ginger
- 2 tablespoons finely chopped garlic
- 6 scallions, sliced
- 1 cauliflower, cut into florets and blanched until barely tender
- 1 tablespoon sugar
- 7 tablespoons **dulse flakes**
- ¼ cup white wine
- 2 tablespoons dry sherry
- 2 tablespoons water
- 2 egg whites, slightly beaten
- 2 teaspoons toasted sesame oil
- 2 teaspoons soy sauce, or to taste
- 1 teaspoon freshly ground black pepper, or to taste

Heat a wok or heavy skillet. Add the peanut oil, ginger, garlic, and scallions. Stir-fry briefly until fragrant. Stir in the cauliflower, sugar, dulse, white wine, sherry, and water. Add the egg whites and cook a few seconds until just set. Remove from the heat and stir in the toasted sesame oil and soy sauce. Serve with freshly ground black pepper to taste.

Per serving: Calories 84, Protein 3 g, Fat 5 g, Carbohydrates 7 g, Fiber 2 g, Calcium 30 mg, Sodium 185 mg

Cooking tip—Greens and Wild Laver

When steaming kale, collard greens, or other land greens, add a strip of **laver** *during the last 2 minutes of steaming. This adds a nice flavor to steamed greens.*

Dulse Croquettes

Yield: 4 servings

An exceptional way to serve dulse. Thanks Christina.

½ cup **dulse**, soaked briefly and diced
½ cup rolled oats
3 or 4 green onions, diced
½ cup grated carrot
Spring or filtered water
About ½ cup yellow cornmeal
Dipping sauce (below)
Safflower oil for deep-frying

Ginger Dipping Sauce
1-inch knob of ginger
½ cup spring or filtered water
1 teaspoon soy sauce
2 teaspoons grated daikon

Combine the dulse, oats, green onions, and carrot with enough water to make a stiff batter. Shape into 2-inch rounds or ovals. Pour the cornmeal into a shallow bowl. Coat each croquette in cornmeal, and place on a plate.

To make the sauce, grate the ginger. Gather into a ball and squeeze the ginger to make juice (about 1 teaspoon). Whisk with the sauce ingredients together in a small bowl, and set aside.

Heat about 2 inches of oil in a deep skillet over medium heat. Add the croquettes in batches, and deep-fry until golden, about 2 to 3 minutes per side. Drain on paper towels, arrange on a platter, and serve immediately with the sauce.

Per serving: Calories 111, Protein 4 g, Fat 1 g, Carbohydrates 22 g,
Fiber 4 g, Calcium 25 mg, Sodium 142 mg

Dulse Sushi

Yield: 8 servings

Take it on an outdoor adventure—day-hike, day-sail, kayaking, etc. Pictured on the cover.

2 cups brown rice
4 cups water if simmering, or 2½ to 3 cups water for pressure-cooking
1 cup firmly packed **dulse**
3 tablespoons tahini
½ teaspoon mustard powder
1 tablespoon hot water
½ tablespoon tamari
6 to 8 sheets toasted nori

Rinse the rice and simmer for 35 to 40 minutes, or pressure cook for 20 to 25 minutes. (Use larger amounts of water in a jiggle-top pressure cooker or for a softer rice.)

Lightly rinse the dulse, squeeze dry, and finely chop.

Mix the tahini, mustard powder, hot water, tamari, and dulse into a creamy paste. Mix this into the cooked rice. Let the rice stand for about an hour until it is cool enough to handle, but still warm.

To roll the sushi, lay one sheet of nori on a bamboo mat with the bamboo running horizontally, or lay the nori on a cutting board. Place about ½ cup of the rice mixture on the bottom half of the nori. Roll, starting with the end closest to you, pressing the ends inward, and using even pressure. Replace any filling that might fall out. Dampen the last ½ inch of the exposed nori sheet to help seal the roll. Slice into rounds to serve.

Per serving: Calories 180, Protein 6 g, Fat 4 g, Carbohydrates 30 g, Fiber 5 g, Calcium 45 mg, Sodium 140 mg

❖ *Feel free to substitute sushi rice for the brown rice. To cook 2 cups of sushi rice, first rinse it, then let it soak in 3 cups of water for 10 to 20 minutes. Bring to a boil and simmer until the water is absorbed, about 15 minutes.*

❖ *Substitute some sweet brown rice for an equal amount of brown rice.*

❖ *You can also add some sliced vegetables by laying them in a line down the middle of the rice before rolling. Try thinly sliced cucumber, carrots, avocado, bell pepper, etc.*

Nori Potato Rolls

or Shep's Simple Sushi

Necessity being the mother of invention, this recipe evolved when I (or Shep) needed something tasty, attractive, and very easy to prepare for our booth at a natural foods show that I was running solo. Three ingredients, a little hot water, and presto!

Fantastic Foods instant "Stuffed Mashed Potatoes" (either soup cup or boxed)
Toasted nori sheets
Sea Pickles (MCSV) or any sour pickle

Make a stiff potato mix using 1 to 2 tablespoons less water than called for on the box. Allow the mix to cool, refrigerate for 30 minutes, or freeze for 10 minutes. Spread the nori sheet as described in "Dulse Sushi," laying a narrow strip of pickles across the potatoes before rolling and sealing. Cut into ½-inch slices with a sharp, wet knife.

Fried Rice with Wild Laver

Yield: 4 servings

Toasted laver is a good garnish and seasoning for cooked grains. For a creative dish with rice, try this recipe from Montse Bradford.

Large piece freshly grated ginger
1 cup **laver**
½ cup chopped roasted almonds
1 cup diced onions
1 teaspoon sesame oil
½ cup matchstick-size carrot pieces
½ cup diced celery
3 tablespoons soy sauce
2 cups cooked brown rice
3 to 4 tablespoons water

Preheat the oven to 300ºF.

Gather the grated ginger into a ball and squeeze the ginger to make about 2 tablespoons juice.

Toast the laver for 5 to 8 minutes until the laver is crisp. Toast the almonds for 10 to 20 minutes until they become aromatic. Crumble the laver into flakes, and set aside. Let the nuts cool enough to chop by hand, or chop them in a food processor. Set aside for garnish.

Heat a heavy skillet or wok. Sauté the onions in the oil for 5 to 7 minutes. Add the carrots and crumbled laver, and sauté 5 more minutes. Add the celery and 2 tablespoons of the soy sauce, and sauté for 5 minutes. Next add the cooked brown rice, water, remaining tablespoon soy sauce, and the ginger juice. Stir continuously for 2 to 3 minutes. Taste and adjust the seasonings, if needed. Garnish with chopped, roasted almonds just before serving.

Per serving: Calories 287, Protein 11 g, Fat 12 g, Carbohydrates 35 g, Fiber 8 g, Calcium 82 mg, Sodium 793 mg

Roasted Nori & Vegetable Fried Rice

Yield: 8 servings

A high-protein, savory main dish.

- 1 cup **laver**
- 2 tablespoons olive oil or peanut oil
- ½ teaspoon toasted sesame oil
- 8 cloves garlic, sliced
- 2 carrots, diced
- 1 onion, diced
- 3 green onions, thinly sliced
- 2 cups chopped broccoli
- 6 cups cooked rice
- 1 to 2 tablespoons soy sauce, or to taste
- 1 tablespoon crushed ginger (optional)

Preheat the oven to 300°F. Toast the laver for 5 to 8 minutes until crisp, or dry roast it in a medium skillet, turning occasionally until crisp.

Heat a wok or heavy skillet. Add the olive oil and toasted sesame oil. Add the garlic and vegetables, and sauté for 3 minutes. Add the rice and toasted laver, and mix thoroughly. Add the soy sauce and ginger, and sauté on medium heat until well mixed. Add more oil if necessary to prevent sticking. Adjust the flavors; add more soy sauce, ginger, and/or garlic, if desired.

Per serving: Calories 241, Protein 7 g, Fat 5 g, Carbohydrates 42 g, Fiber 6 g, Calcium 43 mg, Sodium 215 mg

❖ *Other diced vegetables can be added or substituted—rutabaga, zucchini, potatoes, green beans, cabbage, or whatever you have on hand. Bean sprouts can be added at the last minute.*

Wild Rice Pilaf with Dulse

Yield: 6 to 8 servings

Susan created this great dish with wild rice that combines beautifully with shiitake mushrooms and dulse.

½ pound wild rice (1 cup)
3 cups or more spring water
½ pound long grain rice, rinsed (1 cup)
2 tablespoons plus 1 teaspoon extra-virgin olive oil
2 large leeks, rinsed, trimmed, and thinly sliced
8 large, fresh shiitake mushrooms, sliced in half
3 scant tablespoons **dulse flakes**
Freshly ground black pepper to taste

Cover the wild rice with 3 cups spring water. Bring to a boil, lower the heat, cover, and simmer for 25 minutes. Add the long grain rice, bring to a second boil, cover, and steam another 20 minutes. (Liquid proportions will vary with the age and variety of the rice.)

Heat a heavy skillet, add 2 tablespoons of the olive oil, and sauté the leeks until tender but still bright green. Remove from the skillet and set aside. Add 1 teaspoon more oil, and sauté the mushrooms until they release their moisture.

When the rice is cooked, stir in the dulse flakes, black pepper, and shredded leeks. Garnish with the mushrooms. Serve hot or at room temperature.

Per serving: Calories 153, Protein 3 g, Fat 5 g, Carbohydrates 25 g, Fiber 2 g, Calcium 35 mg, Sodium 96 mg

Sea Palm Fronds Sautéed with Butter & Garlic

Yield: 4 servings

Wow! This is delicious as an appetizer, garnish, or side dish. Thanks Eleanor.

1 cup **sea palm fronds**
1 to 1½ cups water
2 cloves garlic, crushed
2 tablespoons butter
Soy sauce
Lemon juice (optional)

Freshen sea palm fronds by soaking them in the water for 20 minutes. Reserve the soaking water. Separate the fronds and sauté for 3 minutes with the garlic in the butter. Add 1 cup of the soak water, cover, and simmer for about 15 minutes until tender, adding more water if necessary. Add soy sauce to taste and a few drops of lemon juice just before serving.

Per serving: Calories 70, Protein 1 g, Fat 6 g, Carbohydrates 3 g, Fiber 2 g, Calcium 63 mg, Sodium 287 mg

Maine Spring Pasta Primavera

Yield: 4 to 6 servings

A tasty spring green dish that is pictured on the cover.

1 ounce or 1 cup tightly packed **alaria** (midribs removed if desired) rinsed and snipped into 2-inch strips

Sauce
½ cup tahini
2 tablespoons lemon juice
1 teaspoon mixed thyme and basil
2 large cloves garlic, chopped
1 to 2 cups alaria cooking liquid, more as needed

¾ pound fresh fiddlehead ferns, cleaned and cut into 2-inch lengths
1 small fresh hot chile pepper, seeded and chopped
1 cup broccoli florets
1 cup 3-inch pieces fresh asparagus spears
2 small carrots, finely sliced
2 cups fresh or frozen green peas
1 pound fettuccine or linguine
1 tablespoon olive oil
A large handful of fresh chopped herbs in season

Simmer the alaria in enough water to cover for 20 minutes or until tender. Drain and reserve the cooking water.

Combine the sauce ingredients in a blender, and set aside. You can add some alaria cooking water later if it thickens upon standing.

Bring a large pot of water to a boil. Blanch each vegetable except the peas. Briefly plunge the fiddleheads into boiling water for 15 to 30 seconds until they turn bright green. Remove them from the pot with a strainer spoon. Repeat for each vegetable except the peas. Place the blanched vegetables, alaria, and peas in a large bowl.

Bring the water back to a boil. Add the pasta and cook until al dente. Drain, saving 1 cup of water. Put the pasta back in the pot. Add the oil and stir the sauce. Add the reserved alaria stock if necessary to thin the sauce.

Add the vegetables and alaria to the pasta, then add the sauce and combine gently. Add a few tablespoons of reserved cooking water if necessary. Reheat the mixture briefly in the pasta pot, and serve garnished with fresh herbs.

Per serving: Calories 410, Protein 17 g, Fat 16 g, Carbohydrates 55 g, Fiber 12 g, Calcium 199 mg, Sodium 324 mg

❖ *You could substitute string beans or asparagus for the fiddleheads.*

Sea Palm Pasta

Soak the **sea palm fronds** for 20 minutes, then steam for 15 to 20 minutes until the fronds are al dente. Alternatively, cook the fronds as you would pasta in a generous amount of boiling water, "shocking" fronds with a cup of cold water each time they return to a boil. Repeat until the fronds are al dente. Use alone or mixed with pasta, topped with your favorite sauce, or dressing. Garnish with your favorite seeds or nuts.

Sautéed Wakame

Yield: 4 servings

Easy and versatile, you can serve this as a simple side dish or add vegetables and tofu to make it a hearty main dish. Thanks Eleanor.

1 cup dried **wakame** (½ ounce)
2½ cups cold water
1 tablespoon cooking oil
2 tablespoons soy sauce
1 teaspoon crushed ginger root
2 large cloves garlic, crushed
1 tablespoon honey
Hot pepper oil or toasted sesame oil to taste (optional)

Soak the wakame in the water for 10 minutes. Slice the freshened wakame into thin strips. Reserve the water.

In a wok, combine the oil, soy sauce, ginger, garlic, and honey. Sauté for half a minute. Add the wakame and 1½ cups of the wakame soaking water. Simmer for 15 to 20 minutes. Add the hot oil and/or sesame oil. Serve over rice. (Save leftover wakame water for cooking rice or soup.)

Per serving: Calories 68, Protein 2 g, Fat 4 g, Carbohydrates 7 g,
Fiber 2 g, Calcium 63 mg, Sodium 728 mg

❖ *Add onions, carrots, green beans, and/or tofu.*

❖ *Leftovers become marinated wakame, to be served cold as a condiment with hot rice and other dishes.*

Putanesca Sauce with Laver

*Yield: about 3 cups of sauce (enough for
½ pound dry spaghetti—2 to 4 servings)*

*Laver, also known as wild nori, is an excellent substitute for anchovies in this
wonderful vegetarian putanesca sauce. Thanks Susan.*

1⅓ cups tightly packed **laver** (⅔ of a 2-ounce package)
One 28-ounce can diced or crushed tomatoes
2 tablespoons olive oil
4 cloves garlic, smashed
¼ cup hot red pepper flakes, or more to taste
1 small or medium red bell pepper, thinly sliced
2 teaspoons dried basil
1 teaspoon dried rosemary
A large handful fresh basil (or parsley if basil is not in
    season), chopped
Freshly ground black pepper

Preheat the oven to 300ºF. Toast the laver for 5 to 8 minutes until
crisp, or dry roast it in a medium skillet, turning occasionally
until crisp. Crumble into flakes and put in a large mixing bowl.
Add the tomatoes and marinate for 10 minutes or more.

Heat a large saucepan. Add the oil, garlic, hot pepper flakes, bell
pepper, dried basil, and rosemary. Sauté for 5 minutes until the
bell peppers are soft. Add the laver and tomatoes. Simmer, stirring occasionally, for 10 to 15 minutes over high heat to reduce
it to a saucy consistency.

Serve over hot whole grain spaghetti cooked to al dente, sprinkle with the fresh basil, and serve. This dish can be refrigerated
for a few days or frozen.

Per serving: Calories 255, Protein 12 g, Fat 10 g, Carbohydrates 31 g,
Fiber 12 g, Calcium 121 mg, Sodium 485 mg

❖ *For a less rich dish, omit the oil and add garlic, herbs, and peppers
to the simmering tomatoes. Blend for a smooth sauce, then garnish
with olives.*

BEAN COOKERY

Kelp and Beans

In the West, beans have been traditionally flavored with salt pork. In the East, **kelp** or **kombu** has been used. The nutritious, fat-free, vegetarian choice is, of course, kelp.

Kelp provides minerals, trace elements, and phytonutrients without fat or cholesterol. It also contains glutamic acid, the active ingredient in synthetic MSG, but without any side effects. It helps beans cook faster and makes them more digestible. Kelp melts into and thickens the bean sauce, adding rich flavor. It allows reduction of added salt without sacrificing taste.

Choose any dry bean (including slow-cooking dried legumes like peas, lentils, and chick-peas) and your favorite bean cooking method. As you bring the beans to a boil, add kelp or kombu (one 5-inch strip, about ¼ of a 2-ounce bag). The kelp will melt into the bean sauce; the thicker kombu will not. Continue cooking and adding your choice of other ingredients as per your recipe.

Or, if you're cooking bean soup—minestrone, split pea, black bean, lentil, lima—lightly rinse, then rip, chop, or cut the kelp or kombu into bite-size pieces.

You'll get all the nutrition and subtle taste mentioned above. So, if you are already a bean eater, you can become a seaweed eater with virtually no extra effort!

Texas-Style Black-Eyed Peas

Yield: 4 servings

This is an all-American favorite with kelp replacing salt.

- 1⅓ cups black-eyed peas, rinsed and parboiled with enough water to cover
- One 8-inch piece of dried **kelp**, torn into bite-size pieces
- 1 onion, chopped
- 1 teaspoon chili powder
- 2 tablespoons extra-virgin olive oil, or your preferred vegetable oil
- 1 cup chopped tomatoes
- ½ teaspoon **Kelp Granules Sea Seasonings**

Simmer the black-eyed peas and kelp for 30 to 45 minutes until the peas are soft. In a heavy skillet, sauté the onion and chili powder in the oil for 5 minutes. Stir in the tomatoes, kelp granules, and black-eyed peas. Cover and simmer for 10 minutes to blend flavors. Taste and adjust the seasonings.

Per serving: Calories 238, Protein 11 g, Fat 8 g, Carbohydrates 33 g, Fiber 10 g, Calcium 58 mg, Sodium 91 mg

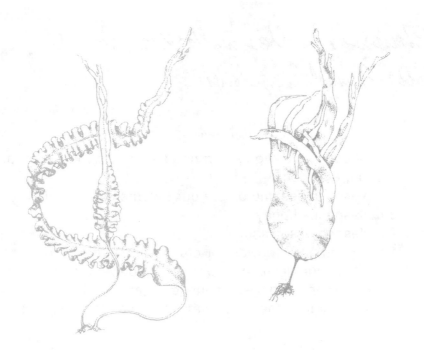

MAIN DISHES

Chinese Noodles with Wakame & Stir-Fried Vegetables

Yield: 4 servings

The whole family will love this for dinner. Thanks Eleanor.

One 4-ounce package Asian noodles (rice noodles, soba, udon, etc.)
1 tablespoon sesame oil or your favorite cooking oil
2 tablespoons honey
2 tablespoons soy sauce
1 teaspoon garlic powder or crushed fresh garlic (optional)
Assorted vegetables, chopped and cubed—carrots, cauliflower, cabbage, onions, etc. (about 4 cups)
½ cup **wakame**, soaked in water to cover, then cut in thin strips
1 pound tofu, cubed
1 teaspoon curry powder
1 teaspoon toasted sesame oil
Thai chile sauce (optional)

Cook the noodles according to package directions.

Meanwhile, heat a wok or heavy skillet, and add the sesame oil, honey, soy sauce, garlic, chopped vegetables, wakame, carrots, and cauliflower. Sauté for 5 to 10 minutes until the vegetables are as tender as you like, and then add the tofu. Stir-fry for 5 minutes or until the tofu absorbs the vegetable flavors and is well coated. Stir in the curry powder. Taste and adjust the seasonings. Drizzle on the toasted sesame oil and Thai chile sauce. Cover and set aside until the noodles finish cooking.

Drain the noodles and serve topped with individual portions of vegetables.

Per serving: Calories 282, Protein 14 g, Fat 8 g, Carbohydrates 41 g, Fiber 6 g, Calcium 91 mg, Sodium 1205 mg

Southwest Peking Rolls with Smoked Dulse & Ancho Chilies

Yield: 6 rolls (60 pieces)

This gourmet dish was created by Chef Steve Cheatham of the Harvest Co-op in Cambridge, Mass.

2 ancho chilies, seeds removed
4 ounces goat cheese
1 teaspoon minced garlic
1 tablespoon lime juice
2 tablespoons canola oil
2 ounces (1 bag) **smoked dulse**
Twelve 12-inch tortillas
1 head green cabbage, shredded
2 bunches scallions, thinly sliced
4 sheets **nori**, shredded

In a small bowl, cover the ancho chilies with boiling water, and set aside for 10 minutes to soften. Drain.

In a food processor, combine the chilies, goat cheese, garlic, and lime juice, and purée until smooth.

Heat the oil in a large sauté pan. Add the smoked dulse in batches, and cook each side until crisp. Cool.

Briefly heat a tortilla in a dry skillet until warm. Spread the chili-cheese mixture on one tortilla. Put another warm tortilla on top with a layer of cabbage, a sprinkling of scallions, and 2 pieces of smoked dulse. Cover with another warm tortilla, and roll tightly, using the chili cheese mixture to hold them together. Cut into 1-inch pieces and top with the shredded nori. Repeat until you use all the tortillas and vegetables.

Per 4 pieces: Calories 163, Protein 6 g, Fat 6 g, Carbohydrates 20 g, Fiber 3 g, Calcium 60 mg, Sodium 320 mg

Dulse Vegetarian Pizza

Yield: 4 to 6 servings

Yahoo! Fire up the oven. This cheese pizza is loaded with dulse. Add your favorite vegetables and have a feast. Pictured on facing page.

12-inch pizza dough (available fresh and frozen at most pizzerias and natural food stores)

1 teaspoon to 1 tablespoon olive oil

3 cups tomato sauce

2 cups grated regular or soy mozzarella

1⅓ cups chopped **dulse**

Assorted thinly chopped vegetables (broccoli, peppers, mushrooms, onions, garlic, olives) and/or seitan

Oregano, basil, and hot pepper to taste

Preheat the oven to 425°F. Lay the dough on a lightly oiled pizza pan. Poke holes gently with a fork all over the dough. Bake for 6 to 8 minutes. Lift the bottom up with a fork, and when it is slightly brown, remove it from the oven. Spread on the tomato sauce and half the cheese. Next spread the dulse and your choice of vegetables and herbs on top, and cover with the rest of the mozzarella. Bake for 10 to 20 minutes until the cheese is melted throughout.

Per serving: Calories 453, Protein 21 g, Fat 18 g, Carbohydrates 55 g, Fiber 9 g, Calcium 325 mg, Sodium 1321 mg

Shepherd's Pie

Yield: 4 to 6 servings

Dulse and nori enrich the flavor and nutrition of this classic dish—one of Shep's favorites.

> 4 to 6 medium potatoes, rinsed
> ½ cup (½ ounce) firmly packed **dulse**, plus a few extra strips
> 2 tablespoons soy margarine or butter
> ¼ to ½ cup soymilk
> Freshly ground black pepper
> 1 large onion, chopped
> 2 tablespoons olive oil
> 1 cup sliced fresh shiitake mushrooms
> 1 pound tofu, drained well and mashed
> 1 tablespoon **Nori Granules Sea Seasonings**
> 1 tablespoon garlic powder
> 1 tablespoon nutritional yeast flakes
> 2 tablespoons soy sauce
> 1 tablespoon corn or canola oil
> 1 cup organic tomato sauce
> 1 fresh tomato or a hand full of dried tomatoes

Boil and simmer the potatoes and dulse until the potatoes are tender, about 20 minutes.

Preheat the oven to 375ºF. Drain and mash the potatoes and dulse with the soy margarine, soymilk, and pepper. Set aside.

Sauté the onion in the oil for 5 minutes. Add the mushrooms and sauté another 5 minutes. Add the tofu and nori granules, and cook another 5 minutes, adding a tad of oil or water if the pan dries out. Stir in the garlic powder, nutritional yeast, soy sauce, and more pepper to taste. Remove from the heat.

Oil a casserole dish and pour in the tofu-mushroom mixture, then about 1 cup tomato sauce and the potato-dulse mixture. Top with slices of fresh tomato or some lightly rinsed dried tomato slices and nice pieces of dulse fully laid out. Bake for 20 to 30 minutes.

Per serving: Calories 439, Protein 22 g, Fat 21 g, Carbohydrates 46 g, Fiber 8 g, Calcium 222 mg, Sodium 824 mg

Apple Kanten and Cherry Kanten (page 152) and (Mocha Custard (page 153) pictured to the left.

Tofu with Laver

Yield: 2 to 4 servings

This stir-fry is loaded with so many minerals, I wanted to call it "Pure Energy." Tofu and laver complement a grain dish for lots of high-quality protein. Thanks Linnette.

¼ package (¼ ounce) **laver**
1 medium onion, diced
1 teaspoon to 1 tablespoon sesame or olive oil
1 pound firm or extra-firm tofu, drained and mashed
1 to 2 cloves garlic, diced very small
One 4-ounce package fresh shiitake, ½ cup dried shiitake, or 1 cup chopped regular mushrooms
Tamari
Freshly ground black pepper
1 bunch watercress, or 8 ounces spinach, chopped (optional)
½ teaspoon to 1 teaspoon ginger, diced very small

Pull apart the laver. Fry over medium heat for 4 to 5 minutes until crisp, pressing occasionally with a spatula or spoon until crumbly. Or set in 300°F toaster oven for 5 to 8 minutes. Set aside.

Sauté the onion in a lightly oiled pan until translucent. Add the tofu, garlic, and mushrooms. (If you are using dried shiitake, reconstitute them by soaking in hot water for 15 minutes then drain.) Sauté until the tofu has lost excess water. Crumble the laver and mix into the pan.

Add tamari and pepper to taste. Mix in optional greens and/or ginger.

Per serving: Calories 284, Protein 26 g, Fat 15 g, Carbohydrates 17 g, Fiber 6 g, Calcium 322 mg, Sodium 28 mg

❖ *Add sliced red bell pepper and/or grated carrot for more color and a fuller dish. You can also add more garlic, ginger, and other types of mushrooms—white button, crimini, portobello, or oyster.*

Try tofu scrambled with toasted laver on toast for breakfast or snacking.

Turkish Dolmas

Yield: 4 servings as side dish, 2 as main dish

Kelp takes the place of grape leaves in this recipe. The shape and elusive sweetness of kelp inspired this recipe. The kelp becomes tender and the filling has a delightful tangy and salty flavor. Leftovers are great served cold, even after a few days. Thanks Susan.

4 ounces **kelp**, inspected for small shells, not rinsed
1 cup chopped green onions
3 cloves garlic, thinly sliced
¼ cup olive oil
2 cups cooked short grain rice, cooled
¼ cup chopped fresh dill
¼ cup chopped fresh mint
Pinch of salt
Freshly ground black pepper
½ teaspoon cinnamon
½ to 1 teaspoon paprika
¼ cup fresh lemon juice
3 tablespoons pine nuts, toasted (optional)
3 cloves whole garlic, peeled
1 lemon, sliced
2 tablespoons lemon juice
Dill and lemon slices, for garnish

With scissors, cut 8 squares of kelp 6 x 6 inches each. (Save the trimmings for bean cookery.)

In a large skillet, sauté the green onions and sliced garlic in half of the olive oil until soft. Add the rice, herbs, spices, lemon juice, and toasted pine nuts.

Place about ¼ cup of the mixture in the center of each kelp square. Fold into a neat package, and tie with kelp strips or dental floss. Place the folded squares in the skillet, and add water to come halfway up the "dolmas." Add the whole garlic and sliced lemon, cover, and simmer gently for 40 minutes. Add the remaining olive oil, 2 tablespoons lemon juice, and garnish with lemon wedges and fresh dill. Serve immediately or keep covered in cool spot until ready to serve.

Per serving (4): Calories 302, Protein 7 g, Fat 14 g, Carbohydrates 38 g, Fiber 10 g, Calcium 298 mg, Sodium 1270 mg

Hiziki Strudel

Yield: 6 to 8 servings

Cooking for people who are not necessarily attracted to sea vegetables can be quite a challenge. Jim, a friend of mine, came up with this dish and so far, no one has been able to resist the rich sautéed vegetables and hiziki wrapped in a flaky pastry crust. Thanks 7.

1 teaspoon light sesame oil
1 cup **hiziki**, soaked until tender (about 10 minutes), and drained
½ teaspoon mirin
Spring or filtered water
1 onion, cut lengthwise into thin slices
1 cup matchstick-size carrot pieces
Soy sauce
Strudel dough
Sesame seeds

Strudel Dough
1 cup whole wheat pastry flour
½ cup yellow cornmeal
Pinch of sea salt
¼ cup corn oil
About 2 tablespoons spring or filtered water

Heat the sesame oil in a skillet over medium heat. Add the hiziki and cook, stirring, for about 4 minutes. Add the mirin and enough water to cover halfway, and simmer over low heat for 20 minutes. Add the onion and carrots, and season lightly with soy sauce. Cover and simmer 10 more minutes. Remove the cover and cook until any liquid has been absorbed. Transfer to a bowl and set aside to cool while preparing the strudel dough.

Sift together the flour, cornmeal, and salt into a bowl. Stir in the corn oil with a fork until crumbly. Slowly add enough water so the dough just holds together. Gather into a ball and knead 2 to 3 minutes.

Preheat the oven to 350ºF. Lightly oil a baking sheet. Roll out the dough between sheets of waxed paper into a thin rectangle. Remove the top sheet of paper, and spread the hiziki filling over the pastry, leaving about 1 inch of dough exposed at the edges all around. Roll, jellyroll style, using the paper to help roll. Seal the ends of the strudel with a fork. Gently transfer to a prepared baking sheet. Cut several slits in the top of the strudel so it will not split during baking. Sprinkle with sesame seeds.

Bake for about 35 minutes until golden. The strudel should sound hollow when tapped. Cool about 10 minutes before slicing. Cut into 1-inch thick slices, arrange on a platter, and serve warm.

Per serving: Calories 204, Protein 4 g, Fat 10 g, Carbohydrates 25 g,
Fiber 5 g, Calcium 45 mg, Sodium 127 mg

Cholent

Yield: 4 to 6 servings

Here are two ways to cook this tasty dish—pressure cooking and simmering. The strip of kelp melts into the stew, creating a wonderful thick sauce. Thanks Linnette.

1 cup pinto beans
1 cup barley
One 4-inch strip **kelp**
8 cups water
1 large onion, diced
2 medium potatoes, cut into ¾ to 1-inch chunks
1 large carrot, cut into ¾ to 1-inch chunks
2 tablespoons mugi (red barley) or chick-pea miso
1 large clove garlic, crushed
Black pepper to taste
Herbs to taste (oregano, thyme, rosemary) (optional)
Nutritional yeast flakes (optional)

To pressure cook: Pick over the beans and discard any broken or shriveled ones you find. Rinse the beans well and put them in a pressure cooker with water 1 inch over the beans. Bring to a boil and let boil 10 minutes or so. (This is a quick soak method used instead of soaking the beans overnight.)

Rinse the barley in a large pot, stirring constantly, through several changes of water until the water runs clear. Inspect the kelp and remove any small shells. Add the kelp to the barley in the pot with the 8 cups of water, and bring to a low boil. Add the onion to the pot.

Add the potatoes and carrot to the pressure cooker. Lock the lid in place, and turn the flame on high. Bring it up to pressure, and cook over low heat for 45 minutes to 1 hour. Turn off the heat and let the pressure come down naturally. Open the lid and taste the beans and barley. If they need more cooking, simmer covered over low heat. Add more water if needed. The stew should be thick.

Add the miso, garlic, black pepper, herbs, and nutritional yeast. Simmer the stew a few minutes to blend the flavors, and serve.

To Simmer: Soak the pinto beans overnight. Drain the soaking water and rinse the beans through at least 3 changes of fresh running water. Put the beans in a pot with 4 cups fresh water and the kelp. Simmer for 45 minutes. Skip this step if using canned or precooked beans.

Rinse the barley in a separate pot. Add it to the bean pot with 3 cups water, and simmer. Chop the vegetables, then add them to the pot with the minced garlic. Simmer for 20 to 25 minutes until the barley is well cooked and the vegetables are tender. Add the miso, pepper, thyme, and nutritional yeast. Simmer a few more minutes to blend the flavors. Taste and adjust the seasonings, if desired.

Per serving: Calories 277, Protein 11 g, Fat 1 g, Carbohydrates 57 g, Fiber 124 g, Calcium 75 mg, Sodium 371 mg

Sea Palm with Carrot Sauce

Yield: 6 servings

Thanks Betsy Holliday and Julia Ferre.

Filling
1 pound tofu
Pinch of sea salt
1 teaspoon basil
½ teaspoon oregano
1 ounce **sea palm fronds**, rinsed and soaked

Sauce
1 large onion, diced
1½ pounds carrots, cut diagonally into 3-inch lengths
3 tablespoons umeboshi plum paste
Pinch sea salt

Topping
⅓ cup toasted sesame seeds
Soy sauce
Chopped parsley

Mash the tofu and mix with the salt and herbs, and set aside.

To prepare the sauce, take enough sea palm soaking water to fill a pressure cooker up to about 1½ inches. First place the onions , then the carrots in the pressure cooker with a pinch of sea salt. Bring up to pressure and cook for 10 minutes. Reduce the pressure and purée the mixture with the plum paste for a mock "tomato sauce" flavor.

If you do not have a pressure cooker, you can simmer the ingredients in a stockpot until tender, 10 to 20 minutes.

Drain the sea palm and reserve the rest of the soaking water. Cut the sea palm into 2-inch lengths, and simmer with enough water to cover, using the soaking water and more if needed. Cook on medium-low for 20 minutes. Add the mashed tofu, stir, cover, and cook while you make the sesame topping. Grind the sesame seeds to a paste in a suribachi or blender. Add a few drops of the soy sauce and enough water to make a thick sauce.

Stir the tofu and sea palm to break up the curds, and cover with the carrot sauce. Top with the sesame sauce and chopped parsley, and cook together for 10 minutes before serving. Adjust salt as needed.

Per serving: Calories 225, Protein 16 g, Fat 10 g, Carbohydrates 22 g, Fiber 8 g, Calcium 293 mg, Sodium 566 mg

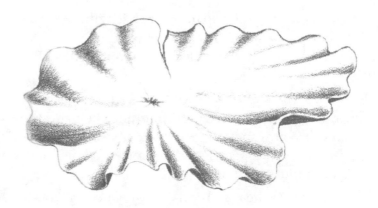

Chinese Three Treasure Stir-Fry

Yield: 6 servings

Three sea vegetables make this stir-fry especially delicious and nutritious, especially served over hot rice. Thanks Susan.

½ cup **laver**
½ cup **alaria**
½ cup **kelp**
2 tablespoons peanut or light sesame oil
2 teaspoons sugar or honey, or 1 tablespoon mirin
2 tablespoons grated fresh ginger
1 large clove garlic, minced
2 red bell peppers, cut into small squares
8 dried shiitake mushrooms, soaked for 10 minutes in hot
  water and cut in half
1½ pounds firm tofu, cut in 6 slices
1 teaspoon 5-spice powder
6 scallions, sliced lengthwise
1 tablespoon soy sauce
2 teaspoons toasted sesame oil

Preheat the oven to 300°F. Toast the laver for 5 to 8 minutes until crisp, or dry roast it in a medium skillet, turning occasionally until crisp.

Cut the dry alaria and kelp into 1-inch lengths. Pressure cook for 15 minutes, or simmer in enough water to cover for ½ hour. Reserve the stock. You should have about 2 cups of sea vegetables.

Heat a wok or large heavy skillet. Add the peanut oil, sugar, ginger, and garlic. Stir-fry until fragrant, then add the red peppers, mushrooms, and tofu. Stir-fry for 1 minute, and add the sea vegetables, 2 tablespoons stock, 5-spice powder, and scallions. Stir-fry a minute or two.

Remove from the heat and add the soy sauce and toasted sesame oil. Serve immediately over rice.

Per serving: Calories 266, Protein 20 g, Fat 16 g, Carbohydrates 15 g,
Fiber 6 g, Calcium 282 mg, Sodium 344 mg

Covered Casserole

Yield: 4 servings

East meets West in this tasty dish. You can substitute other sea veggies if you like, such as kombu, sea palm, and hiziki.

8 cups of assorted veggies (choose 3 to 7 different kinds), cut into bite-size chunks, such as:

1 or 2 varieties of winter squash such as delicata, or butternut squash

root vegetables such as carrot, turnip, daikon, burdock, parsnip, onion

hearty vegetables such as cabbage, leeks, sweet potatoes, yams

fresh or dried mushrooms such as white button, crimini, shiitakes, portobello, morel, maitake, oyster

3 or 4 cloves garlic, diced (optional)

One 5- to 6-inch strip **kelp**

One 1- to 2-inch knob ginger, sliced (optional)

1 cup water

Scallions, parsley, edible flowers, and/or snippets of greens: mizuna, mustard greens, and arugula, for garnish

Preheat the oven to 375°F. Place the cut vegetables and garlic in a large mixing bowl, and mix them together to evenly distribute the garlic.

Cut the kelp with scissors into 1-inch by 2-inch strips, and put it on the bottom of the casserole dish. Add the vegetables, ginger, and water. Bake for 45 minutes to 1 hour until the vegetables are tender and sweet.

Per serving: Calories 124, Protein 4 g, Fat 1 g, Carbohydrates 31 g, Fiber 7 g, Calcium 93 mg, Sodium 94 mg

❖ *Increase the protein and turn this into a main course by adding tempeh or seitan. You could also marinate cubed tofu in tamari for 10 to 15 minutes, and then work it into the layers. Or garnish with seitan, fried tempeh, or smoked tofu.*

❖ *Add 2 teaspoons toasted sesame oil and 1 teaspoon finely chopped dried hot pepper for a spicy dish. Add more chile pepper to increase the heat.*

❖ *To make a sweet-sour version, add 2 teaspoons rice syrup or honey, 2 teaspoons rice vinegar, and 2 teaspoons tamari.*

The "DLT" (Dulse, Lettuce & Tomato Sandwich)

Yield: 1 serving

For less preparation time, lightly rinse the dulse and add it to this sandwich or any veggie sandwich for a great taste and major mineral boost.

Small handful of dry **dulse**
2 slices regular bread or one large pita
Lettuce
Tomato
Olive oil or your favorite cooking oil
1 tablespoon soy mayonnaise

Pull apart the dulse, remove any tiny shells, and pan fry in an oiled pan until the dulse crisps, turns yellow/green, and smells like bacon. Or bake at 300ºF for 3 to 4 minutes on a lightly oiled tray.

Spread the mayonnaise on the bread. Add lettuce, dulse, and tomato.

Per serving: Calories 177, Protein 6 g, Fat 7 g, Carbohydrates 22 g, Fiber 6 g, Calcium 60 mg, Sodium 421 mg

Vegetable Wrap or Stuffed Veggies

Take an avocado, some tahini, garlic, corn, lemon/lime, a strip or two of dulse or smoked dulse, and mix them together. Then wrap the mixture inside of lettuce leaves, spinach, or cabbage, or stuff into a pita or bell peppers.

DESSERTS

Apple Blueberry Walnut Pie

Yield: One 9-inch pie (6 to 8 servings)

Wendy whipped up this winner. Who doesn't like sweet and salty? Apples and dulse are a natural pair, along with blueberries and walnuts.

Pie crust
1 cup whole wheat pastry flour
1 cup white flour
Dash of salt
8 tablespoons butter (1 stick)
6 to 8 tablespoons very cold water

Filling
8 cups finely chopped apples
1 cup fresh or frozen blueberries
1 cup chopped walnuts
½ heaping cup **dulse**, finely cut with scissors
2 tablespoons whole wheat flour
½ teaspoon cinnamon
½ cup maple syrup
2 tablespoons grated butter (optional)

To make the crust, mix the dry pie crust ingredients in a large mixing bowl. Grate in the butter while cold, occasionally covering the stick with some of the flour and stopping now and then to blend the butter into the dough. Add the water and gather together gently until the dough is like a ball. Put in a cool place while preparing the filling.

Preheat the oven to 450°F. Mix all the filling ingredients together in a big bowl.

Divide the dough into two equal parts. Roll one out to form the bottom crust, and put it in a lightly oiled or buttered pie pan. Add the filling. Roll out the remaining dough, and place on top of the filling. Seal the edges and cut a few slits in the top to let the steam out. Bake for 10 minutes, then lower the heat to 350°F and bake for 40 minutes more.

Per serving: Calories 481, Protein 7 g, Fat 21 g, Carbohydrates 9 g, Fiber 8 g, Calcium 43 mg, Sodium 172 mg

Candied Kelp

The Japanese have been making candy from seaweed for centuries. This is MCSV's own concoction. Prepare to be delighted!

Two to three 5-inch strips **kelp**
¼ cup honey
½ cup water
Approximately 1 cup sesame seeds

Soak the kelp in water until it is very soft. Cut it into desired shapes, enough to fill ½ cup.

Bring the honey and water to a boil. Reduce the heat, add the kelp, and simmer uncovered until almost all of the liquid is gone (1 to 1½ hours). Check frequently, adding a dash of water when needed, and stirring occasionally.

Preheat the oven to 300°F. Arrange the kelp pieces on the sesame seeds, turning to coat both sides. (Try using chopsticks for this.) Bake on a clean cookie sheet at 300°F for 25 to 30 minutes. Halfway through baking, turn over the pieces, and be careful not to scorch the sesame seeds!

Per serving: Calories 217, Protein 7 g, Fat 18 g, Carbohydrates 11 g, Fiber 5 g, Calcium 376 mg, Sodium 122 mg

❖ *Try some maple syrup, barley malt, or rice syrup mixed with the honey.*

❖ *You can substitute ground almonds, pecans, walnuts, or peanuts for the sesame seeds.*

Dulse Fruit Cobbler

Yield: 4 to 6 servings

Dulse, oatmeal, fruit, and butter come together for a scrumptious cobbler.

Bottom layer
½ cup fresh or frozen cranberries
2 cups chopped apples
1 cup blueberries
1 cup chopped pears
1 teaspoon vanilla
⅓ to ½ cup maple syrup
1 teaspoon lemon juice

Top layer
1 cup chopped walnuts
1 cup wheat germ
¼ to ⅓ cup grated butter
½ cup finely chopped **dulse**
⅓ cup oatmeal

Preheat the oven to 400°F.

Mix all the ingredients for the bottom layer together, and put into a greased baking pan.

Mix all the ingredients for the top layer together, and spread on top. Bake for 40 minutes.

Per serving: Calories 502, Protein 11 g, Fat 29 g, Carbohydrates 57 g, Fiber 9 g, Calcium 70 mg, Sodium 158 mg

Indonesian Coral Reef Fruit Medley

Yield: 4 servings

Here is a fruit salad with an exotic twist. Thanks Susan.

½ cup (½ ounce) **alaria**, rinsed and midribs removed
¼ cup lime juice or lemon juice
2 bananas, sliced
2 ripe papayas, peeled, seeded, and cut into 1-inch chunks
2 sweet oranges, sectioned
½ cup chopped unsalted peanuts
½ teaspoon freshly ground black pepper
½ teaspoon ground coriander
Pinch cayenne
½ cup (½ ounce) **dulse**, cut into small pieces and rinsed
1 cup unsweetened coconut

Marinate the alaria in 2 tablespoons of the lime or lemon juice for 24 hours. Drain the alaria. Slice it into bite-size pieces, and place them in a shallow bowl.

In another mixing bowl, mix in the banana, the rest of the lime juice, papayas, oranges, peanuts, black pepper, coriander, cayenne, and dulse. Pour the mixture over the alaria, and cover with the coconut.

Per serving: Calories 641, Protein 12 g, Fat 47 g, Carbohydrates 56 g, Fiber 19 g, Calcium 134 mg, Sodium 188 mg

Apple Pizza

Yield: 4 to 6 servings

One 12-inch pie crust
3 cups applesauce
4 tablespoons **dulse flakes**
1 cup grated fresh apples
1½ cups chopped walnuts or other nut of your choice
2 teaspoons cinnamon
4 tablespoons melted butter

Preheat the oven to 450ºF. Spread on the applesauce and sprinkle the dulse flakes on the pie crust. Cover with the grated apples and chopped nuts. Sprinkle on the cinnamon and drizzle on the melted butter. Bake at 450ºF for 10 minutes, then lower the heat to 350ºF, and bake for 20 more minutes.

Per serving: Calories 647, Protein 14 g, Fat 38 g, Carbohydrates 67 g,
Fiber 8 g, Calcium 95 mg, Sodium 337 mg

Sunny Lemonade

Yield: 1 serving

This sounds bizarre, but Judith Cooper Madlener claims it's an old New England treatment for coughs and colds. That could well be, as many early Irish and Scottish settlers had eaten dulse "back home" and still enjoyed it in the New World. This recipe comes with no guarantee. Good luck!

1 tablespoon **dulse**
1 cup water
1 teaspoon lemon juice
1 teaspoon honey

Soak the dulse in cold water for 10 to 15 minutes, then drain. Boil the drained dulse in fresh water for 20 minutes. Strain out a glassful of liquid, add the lemon juice and honey, and drink while hot. (It's good cold, too).

Per serving: Calories 26, Protein 0 g, Fat o g, Carbohydrates 7 g,
Fiber 0 g, Calcium 4 mg, Sodium 23 mg

Agar

Agar, sometimes called agar-agar or kantan in Japan, is made from several members of the red algae family, usually *Gelidium amansii*. Traditionally these seaweeds were gathered, dried, and taken to the mountains in winter. There they were boiled down to a gelatinous liquid and subjected to alternating freezing and thawing to yield the pure, light gray fibrous material now called kantan (Japanese for "cold sky"). This is the product you usually find in natural food stores as bars, flakes, or powder. Less expensive chemically extracted agar is also available in Asian markets.

Colorless, odorless, and almost tasteless, agar is high in calcium, iodine, trace minerals, and fiber, but contains no calories. It produces a firmer gel that melts less easily than gelatin and is completely vegetarian.

Making desserts with agar is quick and easy. Add 1 tablespoon agar flakes or ½ teaspoon agar powder to a cup of juice, soymilk, or stock. Bring to a boil. Simmer 10 minutes for agar flakes, 5 minutes for agar powder, or until dissolved. Add spices, fruit, or vegetables, chill, and serve.

While agar is used mostly to gel desserts—custards, confections, puddings, parfaits, pie fillings, fruit salad molds, and fruit juices—it can also be used to make refreshing bean aspics or jellied vegetable salads. Good combinations to try are split peas and carrots, or lentils, mushrooms, and celery. To boost nutrition, you can cook beans and/or vegetables with another sea vegetable such as dulse or kelp. Once the beans and vegetables are soft, season to taste with herbs and a salty seasoning, and mix in agar (4 tablespoons of flakes per quart of stock). Cook 10 minutes until the agar flakes are dissolved. Pour into a mold or glass casserole dish. Chill and serve.

Apple Kanten

Yield: 4 servings

Kids of all ages love this refreshing smooth gelatin for dessert. Pictured on page 132.

> 1 quart apple juice
> 4 tablespoons **agar flakes**, or 2 teaspoons **agar powder**
> Slivered almonds, toasted coconut, strawberries, or sliced
>   kiwi, for garnish (optional)

Pour the juice into a medium stockpot. Add and stir in the agar. Bring to a boil and simmer for 5 minutes for powder or 10 minutes for flakes, or until the juice is clear and smooth. Pour into 4 individual dessert bowls or a quart-size glass or ceramic bowl. Let it cool on the counter for 4 hours or refrigerate for 2 hours before serving.

Per serving: Calories 127, Protein 0 g, Fat 0 g, Carbohydrates 31 g, Fiber 2 g, Calcium 37 mg, Sodium 17 mg

❖ *Add fresh sliced strawberries, peaches, pineapple, pears, kiwi, cherries, or blueberries. Place the fruit in a dessert bowl, and pour hot kanten on top. Chill and serve.*

❖ *To make different flavors of kanten, simply change the flavor of juice. For instance, use cherry juice for a cherry kanten. Pictured on page 132.*

❖ *For a creamy custard variation, transfer chilled and jelled kanten to the blender or food processor. Blend with 1 to 2 tablespoons of tahini or almond butter and 1 teaspoon vanilla.*

❖ *For a crunchier dessert, add a few nuts or seeds.*

Mocha Custard

Yield: 6 to 8 servings

Comfort food at its best, this custard made with cashews and almonds can be served in a hollowed-out pear for a dramatic presentation. Pictured on page 132.

½ cup almonds
1 cup cashews
1 quart vanilla soymilk
2 tablespoons arrowroot powder
4 tablespoons **agar flakes**
¼ cup maple syrup
¼ cup grain coffee* or instant coffee granules
2 tablespoons carob powder or cocoa powder
Carob or chocolate shavings, for garnish

Grind the almonds into a fine meal in a food processor. Add the cashews and grind them. Scrape down any nuts on the sides of the bowl. Add ½ cup of the soymilk. Blend for about 30 seconds, and add another ½ cup of the soymilk. Repeat until you have added a total of 2 cups soymilk. Blend about 5 minutes, until smooth and creamy.

Pour the mixture through a strainer into a medium saucepan, using a spoon or rubber spatula to move the ground nut meal aside so the liquid passes through the strainer. Discard the ground nuts in the strainer.

Blend the other 2 cups of vanilla soymilk and arrowroot in the food processor. Add to the mixture in the saucepan along with the agar flakes, maple syrup, grain coffee, and carob powder. Turn on the heat and whisk the mixture to dissolve the carob powder and grain coffee. Simmer over medium-low heat, whisking occasionally for 5 to 7 minutes, or until the agar flakes dissolve. Taste for sweetness and add more maple syrup, if desired. Pour into one large bowl or 6 to 8 individual dessert cups. Cool to room temperature (about 4 hours) before serving. Or refrigerate for about 2 hours to set.

*Grain coffee is a caffeine-free substitute for coffee made from grains like barley, rye, and malt, or chicory, beet, or figs.

Per serving: Calories 302, Protein 9 g, Fat 18 g, Carbohydrates 30 g,
Fiber 5 g, Calcium 70 mg, Sodium 28 mg

Nutritional Analyses of Various Sea Vegetables

	Calories	Fat	Carbohydrate	Protein	Fiber	Calcium	Potassium	Magnesium	Phosphorous	Iron	Sodium
	cal/100g	g/100g	g/100g	g/100g	g/100g	mg/100g	mg/100g	mg/100g	mg/100g	mg/100g	mg/100g
ALARIA (Alaria esculenta)	262	3.6	39.8	17.7	38.5	1,100	7,460	918	503	18.1	4,240
DULSE (Palmaria palmata)	264	1.7	44.6	21.5	33.3	213	7,820	271	408	33.1	1,740
KELP (Laminaria longicruris)	241	2.4	39.3	16.1	32.5	942	11,200	900	423	42.6	4,460
LAVER (Porphyra umbilicalis)	318	4.5	45.1	28.4	30.3	188	2,680	378	408	20.9	1,610
HIZIKI (Hizikia fusiforme)	236	0.8	47.3	10.0	17.0	1,400	14,860		59	29.0	
ARAME (Eisenia bicyclis)	267	1.3	51.8	12.0	7.0	1,170	3,860			12.0	
KOMBU (Laminaria japonica)	259	1.1	54.9	7.3	3.0	800	5,800		150	15.0	
WAKAME (Undaria pinnatifida)	271	1.5	51.4	13.0	4.0	1,300	1,800		260	13.0	1,100
NORI (Porphyra tenera)	322	0.7	45.0	34.0	7.0	470	330**		380	23.0	
ROCKWEED (Ascophyllum nodosum)	241	1.0	52.0	10.0	6.0	4,200	2,300	600	200	50.0	3,700
BLADDERWRACK (Fucus vesiculosis)	276	3.6	54.9	6.0	3.8	2,200	2,260	660	90	36.0	2,710
Recommended Daily Allowances (RDAs)	2,000+	65+	300+	50+	25+	1000 mg	3500 mg	400 mg	1,000 mg	18 mg	2,400 mg

+ These guidelines are set by the USDA and the US Dept of Health and Human Services.

Most nutritional assays for North Atlantic sea vegetables provided by Maine Coast Sea Vegetables

Most nutritional assays for Japanese sea vegetables taken from *Vegetables From the Sea*, S.&T. Arasaki, Japan Publications, 1983.

All assays, particularly iodine, vary widely by season, drying method, storage method, etc.

RDAs are determined by the National Academy of Sciences and subject to periodic revision. See www.nas.edu

g/100g=grams per 100 grams
mg/100g=milligrams per 100 grams
mcg (micrograms)=milligrams per kilogram
100 grams = 3.5 ounces
I.U.=International Units

Nutritional Analyses of Various Sea Vegetables

	Iodine	Manganese	Copper	Chromium	Fluoride	Zinc	Vit. A*	Vit. B$_1$*	Vit. B$_2$*	Vit. B$_3$*	Vit. B$_6$*	Vit. B$_{12}$*	Vit. C	Vit. E
	mg/100g	mg/100g	mg/100g	mg/100g	mg/100g	mg/100g	IU/100g	mg/100g	mg/100g	mg/100g	mg/100g	mcg/100g	mg/100g	IU/100g
ALARIA	16.6	1.02	0.172	0.21	4.3	3.44	8,487	0.558	2.73	10.5	6.23	5.03	5.9	4.92
DULSE	5.2	1.14	0.376	0.15	5.3	2.86	663	0.073	1.91	1.89	8.99	6.6	6.34	1.71
KELP	45.3	1.23	0.148	0.24	3.9	2.86	561	0.549	2.48	3.62	8.63	2.6	4.16	2.71
LAVER	1.4	3.46	0.612	0.12	5.8	4.15	4,286	0.577	2.93	5.92	11.21	17.5	12.03	5.09
HIZIKI	40						150	0.01	0.20	4.6		0.57		
ARAME	98-564						50	0.02	0.02	2.6				
KOMBU	193-471	1.67					430	0.08	0.32	1.8	0.27	0.3	11.0	
WAKAME	18-35	3.05					140	0.11	0.14	10.0		.6*	15.0	
NORI	0.5	2.04					10,000	0.21	1.00	3.0	1.04	13-29	20.0	
ROCKWEED	153.7	23.3	0.21	0.058		1			0.50	18.2			37.5	
BLADDERWRACK	65	6.7	0.3	0.2		1.3								
Recommended Daily Allowances (RDAs)	150 mcg	2 mg	2 mg	12 mcg	1.5 mg	15 mg	5,000	1.5 mg	1.7 mg	20 mg	2 mg	6 mcg	60 mg	30 I.U.

*(Thiamine) *(Riboflavin) *(Niacin) *(Pyrodoxine) *(Cyanocobalamin)

g/100g=grams per 100 grams
mg/100g=milligrams per 100 grams
mcg (micrograms)=milligrams per kilogram
100 grams = 3.5 ounces
I.U.=International Units

Most nutritional assays for North Atlantic sea vegetables provided by Maine Coast Sea Vegetables

Most nutritional assays for Japanese sea vegetables taken from *Vegetables From the Sea*, S.&T. Arasaki, Japan Publications, 1983.

All assays, particularly iodine, vary widely by season, drying method, storage method, etc.

RDAs are determined by the National Academy of Sciences and subject to periodic revision. See www.nas.edu

Leslie Cerier
58 Schoolhouse Road
Amherst, MA 01002
413-259-1695
lescerier@aol.com
http://members.aol.com/lescerier
Local and national lectures and cooking
classes with sea vegetables, nutritional
counseling, kitchen designs, and organic gourmet catering

Maine Coast Sea Vegetables
3 Georges Pond Rd
Franklin, ME 04634
207-565-2907
207-565-2144 fax
www.seaveg.com
E-mail: info@seaveg.com
Certified organic North Atlantic sea vegetables, Plus Sea Seasonings, Sea Chips,
Maine Coast Crunch, and Sea Pickles

Maine Seaweed Company
PO Box 57
Steuben, ME 04680
207-546-2875 phone and fax
www.alcasoft.com/seaweed/
North Atlantic sea vegetables

Rising Tide Sea Vegetables
PO Box 1914
Mendocino, CA 95460
707-964-5663
707-962-0599
Pacific and Atlantic sea vegetables

Ocean Energy
2268 Juan Pablo
Santa Cruz, CA 95062
831-476-4265
Pacific coast sea veggies only

Eden Foods, Inc.
701 Tecumseh Rd.
Clinton, MI. 49236
800-248-0320
517-456-7025 fax
www.edenfoods.com
All Asian sea vegetables

Granum
2414 SW Andover St.
Seattle, WA 98106
206-525-0051 ext. 8
Mostly Asian sea vegetables

Goldmine Natural Foods
7805 Arjonas Drive
San Diego, CA 92126
800-475-3663
858-695-0811 fax
www.goldminenaturalfood.com
Asian and American seaweeeds

Healthy Healing
PO Box 436
Carmel Valley, CA 93924
800-289-9222
www.healthyhealing.com
Atlantic sea vegetables plus recommen-
dations from Linda Page, N.D., Ph.D.

Mountain Ark Trading Company
201 Westgate Parkway
Ashville, N.C. 28806
800-643-8909
828-252-9479 fax
Asian and Atlantic sea vegetables

Natural Lifestyle Supplies
16 Lookout Drive
Ashville, N.C. 28804
828-254-8053
828-253-7537 fax
www.natural,-lifestyle.com
Asian and American sea vegetables

North American Kelp
41 Cross St.
Waldoboro, ME 04572
888-662-5357
www.noamkelp.com
Various seaweed products for growing
plants and feeding animals

Saltwater Farms
PO Box 740
South Freeport ME 04078
800-293-5357
Seaweed-based products for plants
and animals

Source, Inc.
101 Fowler Road
North Branford, CT 06471
800-232-2365
203-488-6474 fax
www.4source.com
Seaweed-based products for horses
and dogs

Bibliography

I. Reference books completely or partially about sea vegetables

Arasaki, Seibin and Teruko, *Vegetables From the Sea* (Tokyo: Japan Publications, 1983)

Balch, James F. , M.D. and Phyllis A., C.N.C., *Prescription for Nutritional Healing* pp. 56 (New York: Avery Publishing Group 1997)

Chapman, V.J., *Seaweeds and Their Uses*, (London: Methuen & Co., 1950)

Fryer, Lee, and Simmons, Dick, *Food Power from the Sea, The Seaweed Story* (New York: Mason/Charter, 1977)

Hanson, Larch, *Edible Sea Vegetables of the New England Coast*, (Maine Seaweed Company, P.O. Box 57, Steuben, ME 04680)

Jack, Alex, *Let Food Be Thy Medicine* pp. 136, 151, 159, 195-197, 226, 234-236, 246, 262 (Becket, MA: One Peaceful World Press, 1999)

Kronhausen, Eberhard, Ed.D., Phyllis, Ed.D. *Formula For Life* pp 85, 151, 152, 157-160, 163, 173-175, 316, 331 (New York: William Morrow, 1989, 1999)

Leigh, Michelle Dominique, *Inner Peace, Outer Beauty: Natural Japanese Health and Beauty Secrets Revealed* (New York: Citadel Press, 1995)

Madlener, Judith Cooper, *The Sea Vegetable Book* (New York: Clarkson N. Potter, 1977)

Magruder, William H., and Hunt, Jeffrey W., *Seaweeds of Hawaii* (Honolulu: Oriental, 1979)

McConnaughey, Evelyn, *Sea Vegetables, Harvesting Guide and Cookbook* (Naturegraph: Happy Camp, CA, 1985)

Page, Linda Rector, N.D., Ph.D., *Healthy Healing, A Guide to Self-Healing for Everyone* pp. 100, 176, 204 (Healthy Healing Publications, 1997)

Powell, Eric F.W., *Kelp: The Health Giver* (Henigscote, Bradford, Holsworthy, North Devon, U.K.: Health Science Press, 1968)

Schechter, Steven R., *Fighting Radiation With Foods, Herbs, and Vitamins* (Brookline, MA: East West Health Books, 1988)

Soule, Deb, *The Roots of Healing, A Woman's Book of Herbs* pp 58, 65-70, 83, 104, 207 (New York, Citadel Press/Carol Communications, 1995)

Taub, Harald J., *Keeping Healthy in a Polluted World*, pp 125, 142, 180, 199-201, New York: Harper & Row, 1974

Weed, Susan S., *Wise Woman Ways: Menopausal Years* (Woodstock, N.Y.: Ash Tree Publishing, 1992)

Yeager, Susan et al, *The Doctors Book of Food Remedies*, pp. 477-481, (PA: Prevention Health Books/Rodale, 1998)

II. Cookbooks completely or partially about sea vegetables

Beasley, Joseph D. and Knightly, Susan, *Food for Recovery* pp. 113-14, 266-67 (New York: Crown Publishers, 1994)

Beling, Stephanie, M.D., *Power Foods*, pp. 30, 85-88, 140, 151, 162, 179 (New York: Harper Collins, 1997)

Bergeron, Ken, *Professional Vegetarian Cooking*, (New York: John Wiley & Sons, 1999)

Berkly, Peter, *The Modern Vegetarian Kitchen* (New York: Harper Collins, 2000)

Bradford, Peter and Montse, *Cooking with Sea Vegetables* (New York: Thorsen Publishing Group, 1985)

Cerier, Leslie *The Quick & Easy Organic Gourmet* (Barrytown: Station Hill Openings, Barrytown Ltd., 1996)

Claffey, Karen *Fast and Fun Food for People on the Go* (Montreal: Karen's Kitchen, 1995)

Colbin, Annemarie, *Food and Healing* pp. 98, 123, 158, 171-172, 180-81, 227, 262, 274, 306-07, (New York: Random House, 1986)

Cousens, Gabriel, M.D. *Conscious Eating* (Santa Rosa, CA: Vision Books International, 1992

DeAngelis, Lissa and Molly Siple, *Recipes for Change, Gourmet Wholefood Cooking for Health and Vitality at Menopause*, pp. 89, 130 (New York: Dutton, 1996)

Ellis, Lesley, *Seaweed, A Cook's Guide* (Tucson, AZ: Fisher Books, 1998)

Karush, Wendy, *Good Food, A Collection of Vegetarian Recipes* (Hancock, ME: Karush, 1996)

Kahn, Barbara, *The Organic Gourmet* pp.227, 65, 67 (Berkeley, CA: Frog Ltd, 1995)

Markowitz, Elysa, *Warming Up to Living Foods* (Summertown, Tennessee: Book Publishing Co, 1998)

McEachern, Leslie, *The Angelica Kitchen* (New York: Roundtable, 2000)

Null, Gary, *The New Vegetarian Cookbook* pp 83-87, (New York: Collier/Macmillan, 1980)

Page, Linda Rector, N.D., Ph.D.,*Cooking for Healthy Healing* (Healthy Healing Publications, 1995)

Pirello, Christina ,*Cooking the Whole Foods Way* (New York: Berkley Publishing Company, 1997)

Rhoads, Sharon Ann, *Cooking with Sea Vegetables* (Brookline, MA: Autumn Press, 1978)

Rogers, Sherry A., M.D., *The Cure is in the Kitchen* (Prestige Publishing, Box 3161, Syracuse, N.Y. 13220)

Thomas, Lalitha, *10 Essential Foods* pp. 42, 84, 134-58 (Prescott AZ: Hohm Press, 1997)

Walford, Roy L., M.D. and Lisa, *The Anti-Aging Plan* pp. 90, 95, 96 (NY: Four Walls Eight Windows, 1994)

MEASUREMENTS & METRIC CONVERSION CHART

Dry Measure Volume Equivalents

1 quart = 4 cups
1 pint = 2 cups
1 cup = 8 fluid ounces
1 cup = 16 tablespoons
1 tablespoon = .5 fluid ounce
1 tablespoon = 3 teaspoons
1 pint = .55 liter
1 quart = 1.1 liters
1 liter = 1.82 pints

Fluid Volume Equivalents

1 teaspoon = 5 milliliters
1 tablespoon = 15 milliliters
1 ounce = 29.56 milliliters
1 quart = .946 liter

Weight Equivalents

1 ounce = 28.35 grams
3.57 ounces = 100 grams
.25 pound = 113 grams
1 pound = 16 ounces
1 pound = 453 grams

Approximate Equivalents

1 fluid ounce = about 28 grams
1 cup cooking oil = 200 grams
1 tablespoon cooking oil = 14 grams
1 cup fluid water = 220 grams
1 tablespoon water = 15 grams
1 cup flour = 100 grams
1 tablespoon flour = 8 grams
1 cup sugar = 200 grams
1 tablespoon sugar = 12 grams

Purchase these classic vegetarian cookbooks from your local bookstore or natural foods store, or you can buy them directly from:

Book Publishing Company

P.O. Box 99

Summertown, TN 38483

1-800-695-2241

www.bookpubco.com

Please include $3.50 per book for shipping and handling

Japanese Cooking
Contemporary &
Traditional
$12.95

Miso Cookery
$10.95

Warming Up to
Living Foods
$15.95

The Shiitake Way
$9.95

The New
Now and Zen Epicure
$19.95